PARASHAH

דְּבָרִים THE BOOK OF DEUTERONOMY

RABBI DANIEL K. ALTER
JOEL LURIE GRISHAVER

TORAH AURA PRODUCTIONS

ISBN 978-1-961607-09-5

Backgrounds: Cover, Introduction (pages 5–8) and Parashat Be-Ha'alotekha (pages 21–27) AlexSurf / Shutterstock; Parashat Be-Midbar (pages 9–14) Happy Person / Shutterstock; Parashat Naso (pages 15–20) Ensuper / Shutterstock; Parashat Shela<u>h</u> Lekha (pages 28–33) Yaroslav Vitkovskiy / Shutterstock; Parashat Kora<u>h</u> (pages 34–41) djero.adlibeshe yahoo.com / Shutterstock; Parashat <u>H</u>ukkat (pages 42–46) Rakaatharf / Shutterstock; Parashat Balak (pages 47–52) Rakaatharf / Shutterstock; Parashat Pin<u>h</u>as (pages 53–57) Art Furnace / Shutterstock; Parashat Mattot (pages 58–63) YamabikaY / Shutterstock; Parashat Masei (pages 64–61) osmak olga / Shutterstock.

Torah Aura Productions (800) BE-Torah • (800) 238-6724 • E-MAIL <misrad@torahaura.com>

Visit the Torah Aura website at www.torahaura.com

MANUFACTURED IN USA

TABLE OF CONTENTS

PARASHAH DEUTERONOMY
A TEACHER'S INTRODUCTION

RABBI DANIEL K. ALTER & JOEL LURIE GRISHAVER

Welcome to Parashah: Experiencing the Weekly Torah Portion!
We designed this workbook for 6th and 7th grade students in
Jewish religious school settings. As these students approach
becoming bat and bar mitzvah, this book intends to demonstrate
the continued relevance and meaning in the mitzvah of *talmud
Torah* - Torah study - by drawing a specific mitzvah or Jewish
value from each Torah portion and directly linking that mitzvah
or value to real world social action. In doing so, we hope to
provide: 1) an outline for creating a *dvar Torah*, and 2) inspiration
for a mitzvah project.

In this book, we break down each of the eleven *parshiot* found
in the book of Deuteronomy into several sections. Each
section approaches the text from a different perspective and
works together to create a whole narrative of one particular
Jewish teaching, from Torah text to rabbinic interpretation to
contemporary action. While each section can be approached and
utilized independently, some supplements may be necessary to
instill the full weight of what they have to offer. Each *parashah*
includes the following sections. All will be found in the following
order, except for Rashi's Commentary and <u>Hevruta</u> Learning,
which jump around as best fits the lesson.

- **OVERVIEW:** The *parashah* overview delineates the book, chapters, and verses included in the Torah portion and provides a short summary of its major plot points. Certain minor interludes or tangents may be glossed over or skipped in order to keep the reader's focus on areas of the text more related to the chosen mitzvah.

- **OUR ToRAH TEXT:** This section highlights a particular verse or set of verses which will serve as a textual basis for the selected mitzvah associated with the *parashah*. The excerpt includes articulated (vowelized) Hebrew text, the Hebrew text as it looks in a Torah scroll (known as k'tav STaM"M), and a good faith translation into colloquial English. Most excerpts include an introductory statement to provide some context or reasoning for the selection.

- **EXPLORING OUR ToRAH TEXT:** In this section, students wrestle with rabbinic commentary, interpretation, or other Jewish texts that help connect the *parashah* to the associated mitzvah. Some parshiot include activity instructions, such as having a class debate or answering discussion questions. Others do not have an attached activity and instead offer additional teachings.

- **RASHI'S COMMENTARY:** This section introduces students to the commentary of Rabbi Shlomo Yitzchaki, better known as Rashi. He is considered a preeminent medieval commentator, providing a solid foundation for engaging with medieval rabbinic commentary. Each Rashi's Read section offers one of Rashi's comments on a particular Torah verse from the *parashah* related to the chosen theme, along with discussion questions or a suggested activity which empower students to go beyond learning the commentary and engage as commentators and interpreters of Jewish text themselves. Rashi intended his commentary to aid the average reader's understanding of Torah. Sometimes, the aid he intends is quite clear. Other times, Rashi answers a question we have not asked. Determining what that question was, what Rashi was

attempting to clarify, can be part of the fun of engaging with his commentary.

- **HEVRUTA LEARNING:** For generations, *hevruta* learning—partnered learning - has been and continues to be the predominant Jewish learning model. In this section, students will engage in *hevruta* learning, often by juxtaposing two or more texts and exploring the dominant themes presented in them. Many chevruta sections include specific discussion questions. Others simply ask students to compare and contrast, leaving space for them to discover and attempt to answer their own questions.

- **ToRAH EXPERIENCE:** The Torah Experience section brings the chosen theme to life by demonstrating its relevance to our students' lives, often through an additional Jewish text and/or a class activity. These experiences empower students to comment and interpret aspects of the *parashah* for themselves, through their own beliefs and life experiences.

- **MITZVAH OF THE WEEK:** This section introduces a new specific and actionable mitzvah or Jewish value, both in Hebrew and English, that is connected to a theme of the *parashah* by defining it and offering a Jewish textual foundation for it. Students then further explore the mitzvah in the following section.

- **MITZVAH EXPERIENCE:** Here, students engage with the mitzvah of the week through research, a Jewish text, or an activity to help it come alive.

- **MITZVAH RESOURCES:** The Mitzvah Resources section offers several websites and organizations relevant to the mitzvah of the week, available for further learning and inspiration, perhaps for an additional class activity or a mitzvah project.

Many sections in this book offer specific classroom activities. When not otherwise specified, we recommend a class discussion format. We encourage student participation, both as readers and as interpreters of our shared text. Making space for student questions

and empowering students to offer their own answers is integral to the *Talmud Torah* experience. Throughout each *parashah*, we have included Reflection Questions. Take inspiration from these to add your own as befits the students you have in your classroom.

For many, studying Torah can feel a little overwhelming. While we do include selected wisdom from Jewish tradition, please do not allow that to impede your or your students' capacity to share your, or their, own wisdom. Judaism teaches that each of us was present for and experienced the moment of revelation at Mt. Sinai. We also teach that every new insight that future students of Torah would introduce were already part of revelation at Sinai (Babylonian Talmud, Megillah 19b, Jerusalem Talmud Peah 13a/2:4). We hope that through this book, our students take another step (or three!) forward toward taking their place beside us as Sinai.

דְּבָרִים DEVARIM

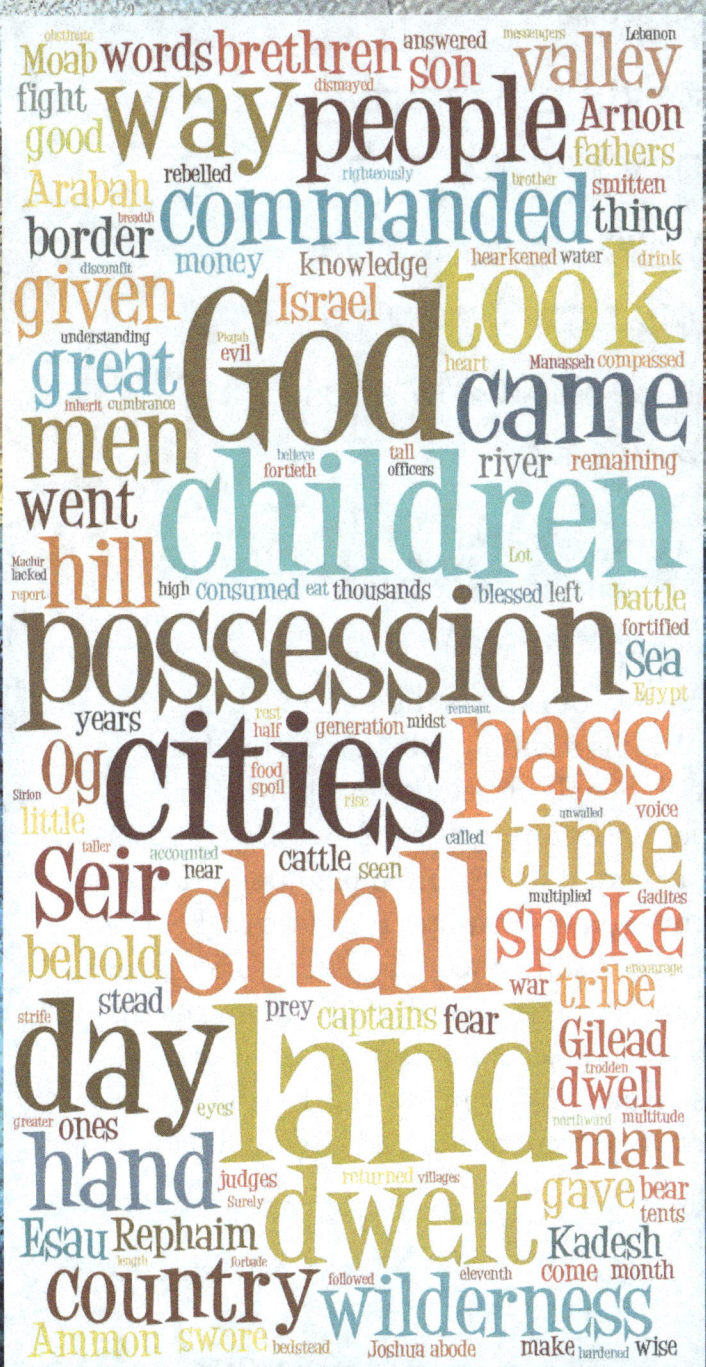

OVERVIEW
DEUTERONOMY 1:1–3:22

The first portion of the last book of the Torah sets up what will occur throughout the book—a review of all that has happened since the Israelites left Egypt. Deuteronomy is Moses' final monologue, a last reminder of everything the Jewish people need to know before they continue their journey into the land of Israel without him.

This *parashah* specifically reviews the Israelites' journey from Sinai to Kadesh, the appointment of assistants for Moses, the journey to Horeb and then to Kadesh-Barne'a, the people's refusal to enter the Land of Canaan and the allotment of conquered land.

9

OUR ToRAH TEXT: DEUTERoNOMY 1:1

Our *sidrah* begins with Moses getting ready to die. He begins to reteach the whole Torah to the Jewish people.

אֵלֶּה הַדְּבָרִים אֲשֶׁר דִּבֶּר מֹשֶׁה
אֶל־כָּל־יִשְׂרָאֵל בְּעֵבֶר הַיַּרְדֵּן...

אלה הדברים אשר דבר משה
אל כל ישראל בעבר הירדן

These are the things that Moses said to all of Israel from across the Jordan River...

RASHI'S COMMENTARY

What does "from across the Jordan River" mean? Who is standing where, exactly? Have the Jewish people already crossed the river?!? Rashi does not comment on it, but his grandson, **Rashbam** (aka **R**abbi **Sh**imon **b**en Meir), does! Rashbam explains that our Torah text takes the perspective of someone living in the land of Israel. Therefore, "across the Jordan River" means the outside, the east side. Look at a map of Israel to see this visually. Why might the Torah take the perspective of someone already living in Israel?

EXPLORING OUR ToRAH TEXT

Read the following *midrash* then discuss: what Jewish practice is suggested here?

> When God informed Moses that he would die after battling Midian, Moses requested, "Please, God, permit me to review the entire Torah with the people before my passing! I wish to clarify any difficulties they may have and to acquaint them thoroughly with the details of the Torah laws."
>
> The Almighty honored Moses' request. On the first day of the month of Shevat, 2488, thirty-seven days before Moses' death, God told him, "Assemble the people to review the mitzvot with them, and to instruct them in those mitzvot they have not yet heard from you."
>
> Moses himself had learned all the mitzvot from God either at Mt. Sinai or in the first year after that in the Tent of Meeting *(Deuteronomy Rabbah 1:6).*

ToRAH EXPERIENCE

Deuteronomy may have been the very first example of an ethical will. An ethical will is a collection of your wisdom and learned experience that you leave for your family and friends.

Check out this ethical will on YouTube: John from North Olmsted shares his Legacy *http://www.youtube.com/watch?v=E2XEpmso4tY*

Take a few minutes to brainstorm one piece of wisdom that you have learned over your lifetime, something that you have found meaningful or helpful. As a class, create a venue to share your collected wisdom, such as a book, a video, a poster, or a website!

Reflection Question: What did it feel like to share a piece of wisdom with others? From whom would you like to receive an ethical will?

MiTZVAH OF THE WEEK: שׁוֹפְטִים *SHOFTiM*

There are two *mitzvot* in this *parashah* that address the qualifications for judges. A rabbi was not only a teacher but could be a judge. Judaism wants courts to help people act appropriately and be good people. If courts were that important, those who served as judges were equally important.

In this *sidrah*, we learn some of the qualifications of a good judge: (a) knowing the Law, (b) knowing Torah, (c) being modest, (d) feeling awe in God, (e) being respected by others, (f) being a seeker of truth, (g) not taking bribes, and (h) not being afraid of litigants.

Is there anything you would add to this list of qualifications?

Reflection Question: What is the difference between qualifications A and B above?

HEVRUTA LEARNING:

The rabbis of the Talmud add to the Torah's list of qualifications for being a judge. Read the following excerpt and discuss what value that these new qualifications add:

> Rabbi Yoḥanan says: Judges must be people of high stature, and of wisdom, and of pleasant appearance, and of suitable age so that they will be respected. And they must also be masters of sorcery, and they must know all seventy languages in order that the Sanhedrin will not need to hear testimony from the mouth of a translator.
>
> Rav Yehuda says that Rav says: Judges must know how to evaluate a non-kosher animal as kosher. *(Sanhedrin 17a:21-22)*

Do you agree with the rabbis on all these new requirements? Do you disagree with any?

Why must judges know sorcery? Why must judges know many languages?

Why must judges be able to call a non-kosher animal kosher?

שׁוֹפְטִים *SHOFTIM* EXPERIENCE

Split the class into groups of five. Three students are going to be judges in a Beit Din (a Jewish court); the other two are going to be litigants in a case they make up. In a Beit Din there are no lawyers. The judges do all the questioning. Run as many trials as you have groups. Have the judges work out and share a verdict (after asking all the questions they want).

Sample cases could include:

- A student accuses another student of stealing their lunch money from their backpack. The accused student claims they are innocent.

- A baseball accidentally breaks a window at school, and two students who were playing catch are brought to court. One claims they didn't throw the ball that broke the window, while the other says it was an accident.

- A child accuses another child of stealing their bicycle from outside the school. The accused child denies the allegation, stating they found the bike abandoned in the park.

- A student accuses their classmate of stealing their homework and copying it. The accused student denies the accusation, claiming they completed their own work independently.

- Graffiti appears on the walls of a classroom, and two students are suspected of being involved. One student claims they witnessed the other drawing on the walls, while the accused student denies the accusation, stating they were elsewhere during the time of the incident.

Reflection Question: What is hard about judging?

שׁוֹפְטִים *SHOFTiM* RESOURCES

As long as we are talking about judges (*shoftim*), here are some justice (*mishpat*) resources.

- American Constitution Society http://www.acslaw.org/
- Public Justice Foundation http://www.publicjustice.net/
- Child Rights International Network https://home.crin.org/

וָאֶתְחַנַּן VE-ETHANNAN

OVERVIEW: DEUTERONOMY 3:23–7:11

Our *parashah* begins with one of the most famous scenes in the Torah. Moses is standing on the top of a mountain called Pisgah on the eastern side of the Jordan and is told to look west, north, south and east to view the land that he is not to enter. Although Moses prays to be allowed to enter the Land of Israel, God refuses, and that privilege is left to Joshua. Moses assigns three Cities of Refuge. We review the Sinai experience and the Ten Commandments.

OUR ToRAH TEXT: DEUTERoNOMY 6:4

Along with many *mitzvot*, a section of this *sidrah* has become a common piece of our liturgy. Some people call it the *Shema* and the *V'Ahavta*. Others call it the first paragraph of the *Shema*.

שְׁמַע יִשְׂרָאֵל יהוה אֱלֹהֵינוּ יהוה אֶחָד:

שמע ישראל יהוה אלהינו יהוה אחד

Listen Israel! The Eternal is our God.
The Eternal is one.

RASHI'S COMMENTARY

While the word אֶחָד *ehad* in Hebrew means "one", some translations say "The Eternal alone" instead of what we have above. Rashi seems to like this translation. According to his commentary, this verse means that God is our God and not the God of other nations. However, he does say that one day, God will be the only God, a single God for all peoples of the earth.

Do you agree or disagree with Rashi? Why?

EXPLoR!NG OUR ToRAH TEXT

Open a *siddur* (prayer book) to the *Shema* and the *V'ahavta*. See how many *mitzvot* you can identify within!

TORAH EXPERIENCE

As you may have seen, the *V'ahavta* contains the mitzvot of affixing *mezuzot* and wrapping *tefillin*. As a class, learn how to wrap *tefillin*. How did it feel to wear *tefillin*?

Reflection Question: What could wearing *tefillin* add to the experience of prayer?

MITZVAH OF THE WEEK: אֱמוּנָה *EMUNAH*—FAITH

According to Maimonides, the *Shema* teaches that it is a mitzvah for us to believe in God. Maimonides created a famous list of thirteen things that he thought all Jews should believe. Here are the first few:

The **first** is to believe in the existence of the Creator, who causes everything to exist. The Creator also sustains existence.

The **second** is to believe in the unity of God. In other words, to believe that this being, which is the cause of all, is one. This does not mean one as in one of a pair nor one like a species (that includes many individuals) nor one as in one object that is made up of many elements nor as a single simple object which is infinitely divisible. This is referred to when the Torah says "Listen Israel. The Eternal is our God. The Eternal is one" (Deuteronomy 6:4).

The **third** is that God is not physical. This means to believe that the One whom we have mentioned is not a physical entity, a body. In all places where the Torah speaks of God in physical terms, such as walking, standing, sitting, speaking and anything similar, it is always metaphorical, as our rabbis said, "The Torah speaks in the language of people."

Restate the three big ideas that Maimonides talks about here.

17

ḤEVRUTA LEARNING

Each statement in Maimonides' original list begins the same way: אֲנִי מַאֲמִין *ani m'amin*—"I believe with perfect faith…" What does faith even mean? Sometimes, people talk about blind faith, which means believing in something without any reason or evidence. Does Judaism believe in blind faith? No, and we learn this from the Hebrew language itself!

The Hebrew word for faith is אֱמוּנָה *emunah*. Its root letters are *alef-mem-nun*. א *Alef* is the first letter of the alphabet. Mem is the middle letter, and nun is just one after that. From this, the rabbis teach that faith is based on having the slightest majority—50% plus one—of information on something. It's not blind, but it's not complete either. If we had 100% of information, it would not be faith anymore. It would be truth, which in Hebrew is אֱמֶת *emet:* א־מ־ת *aleph-mem-tav*, the first letter, the middle letter, and the last letter. In other words, the beginning, the end, and everything in between!

EMUNAH EXPERIENCE

Rabbi Jonathan Sacks, the former chief rabbi of Great Britain, once said: "In Judaism, to be without questions is not a sign of faith but a lack of depth." In other words, in Judaism, asking questions, even questions about tough topics like God, are both necessary and important.

With a partner, create a list of questions that you have about God.

Then, join with another *chevruta* pair to form a group of four. Share the questions that you created, and discuss different answers to those questions.

Share any new revelations with the class.

Reflection Question: Why might asking questions be more important than finding answers?

EMUNAH RESOURCES

Take "One God." Add the fact that "all people are created in God's image." That makes every person responsible for everyone else. Here are the sites for several foundations devoted to the idea of one.

- One http://www.one.org/
- 1 World Foundation https://www.1worldfoundationgroup.org/
- One Water https://onewater.org.uk/
- One World One Ocean https://oneworldoneocean.com/
- One World One Heart Foundation https://www.oneworldoneheartfoundation.org/

עֵקֶב EKEV

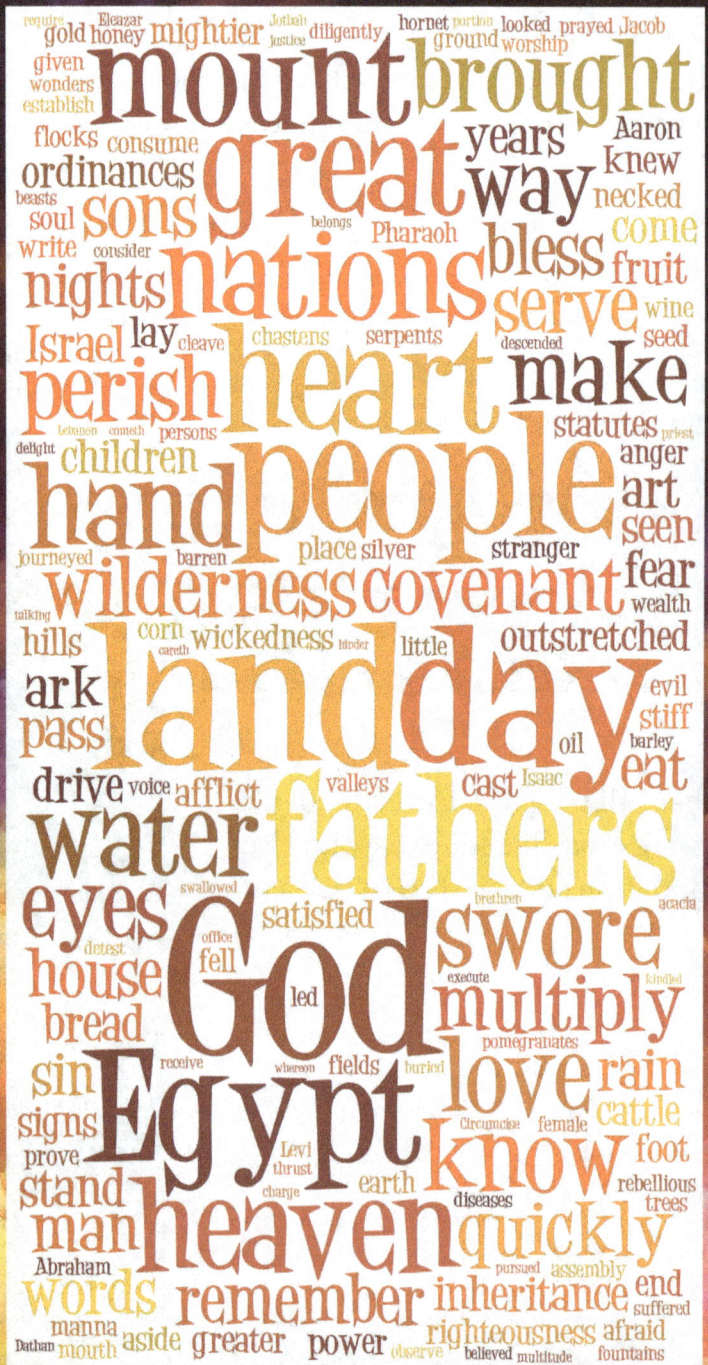

OVERVIEW: DEUTERONOMY 7:12–11:25

Ekev begins with the blessings that come from following God's commandments and the consequences of not following those commandments. Moses reminds the people not to be self-righteous and to learn the lessons of our history: following God's commandments brings us prosperity and health, and our collective memories can affect our relationship with God and *mitzvot*.

OUR ToRAH TEXT: DEUTERONOMY 8:10

This section of Torah talks about rules for what you have to do when you enter the land of Israel and start to live there. We also find a practice that many Jews continue to do multiple times a day!

וְאָכַלְתָּ וְשָׂבָעְתָּ וּבֵרַכְתָּ יי אֱלֹהֶיךָ
עַל־הָאָרֶץ הַטֹּבָה אֲשֶׁר נָתַן־לָךְ:

ואכלת ושבעת וברכת יהוה אלהיך
על הארץ הטבה אשר נתן לך

When you have eaten, and you are satisfied, then you shall bless the Eternal, your God, for the good land that was given to you.

RASHI'S COMMENTARY

Surprisingly, Rashi did not comment on this verse! Some of our other commentators, though, wonder about the phrase עַל־הָאָרֶץ הַטֹּבָה *al ha-aretz tovah*, "for the good land." The Hebrew preposition *al* usually means "on," so does this verse mean that we only need to bless God "on the good land which was given to you" aka the land of Israel? Two commentators, Nachmanides and Rabbi Jacob ben Asher, both say no. They agree that we should bless and thank God no matter where you are, for the good food and for the land on which it grows.

HEVRUTA LEARNING

What does it mean to be "satisfied?" In this case, does it mean eating until you meet your dietary needs? Or eating until you feel full? Or does it mean eating until you have eaten as much as you want to eat? Or does it refer to the taste and texture of the meal?

With your partner, discuss these questions and others that you create yourselves in order to build a definition for the word "satisfied."

Share your definition with another _hevruta_. Can you come to an agreement where all four members are satisfied with the definition?

EXPLORING OUR ToRAH TEXT

From our verse, the rabbis understand the mitzvah to say בִּרְכַּת הַמָּזוֹן _Birkhat ha-Mazon_, the blessings we offer after a meal. That seems pretty straightforward. But we also say blessings _before_ we eat! Where do those come from?

A medieval French commentary known as the Bekhor Shor wrote that the blessing before meals is derived logically: if we bless and thank God for food when we are full and satisfied, all the more so should we bless and thank God for food when we are hungry!

Our Talmudic rabbis took things a step further (Berakhot 35a). They taught that it is prohibited to benefit from anything in the world without offering a blessing on it beforehand. Why? They saw the world and everything that exists on it as belonging to God. By offering a blessing, we are asking God's permission to enjoy it. Without a blessing, the rabbis say, we are stealing it!

ToRAH EXPERiENCE

Birkat ha-Mazon is made up of four blessings. Work with a small group and decide what four things you would want to thank and bless God for after eating.

Reflection Question: What blessings do you have in your life that you show gratitude for every day?

MiTZVAH OF THE WEEK: בְּרְכַּת הַמָּזוֹן *BIRKAT HA-MAZON*

Some Jews offer *Birkhat ha-Mazon* after every single meal. Others offer it when they are at summer camp or other specifically Jewish settings. Still other Jews never offer it. As we have seen, our Torah verse creates the *mitzvah*, or we might say the obligation, to offer *Birkhat ha-Mazon*:

> "When you have **eaten**, and you are **satisfied**, then you shall **bless** the Eternal, your God…".

Reading rabbinically, the message is clear. Step 1: Eat. Step 2: Be nourished. Step 3: Offer *Birkat ha-Mazon*. According to the rabbis, we do not need to eat a full meal to offer *Birkat ha-Mazon*. If we eat something at least the size of an olive, we offer the blessing!

Reflection Question: Why might we use an olive as the minimum size? If you had to create a new minimum amount of food in order to offer the blessing, what would you choose and why?

EXPERIENCING בִּרְכַּת הַמָּזוֹן *BIRKAT HA-MAZON*

As a class, create a *Birkat ha-Mazon* booklet, also known as a bencher.

1. Study some בִּרְכַּת הַמָּזוֹן *Birkat ha-Mazon* booklets.
2. In committees, prepare the text.
3. Make drawings to decorate the pages.
4. Make sure that you copy enough copies.
5. Eat a meal together.
6. Say בִּרְכַּת הַמָּזוֹן *Birkat ha-Mazon* from your booklet.

בִּרְכַּת הַמָּזוֹן *BIRKAT HA-MAZON* RESOURCES

Here are some stop hunger websites.

- Trickle Up http://www.trickleup.org
- Freedom from Hunger
  http://www.freedomfromhunger.org/
- Rise Against Hunger
  https://www.riseagainsthunger.org/

רְאֵה RE'EH

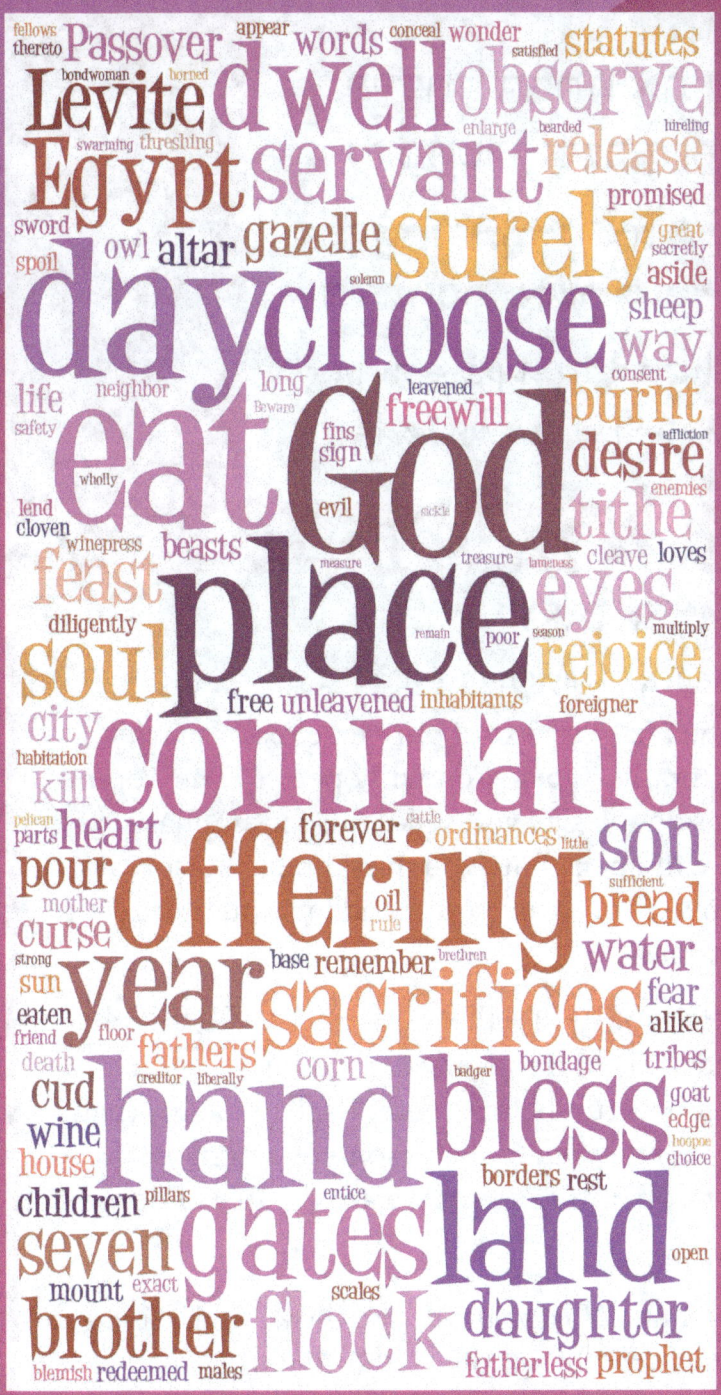

OVERVIEW: DEUTERONOMY 11:26–16:17

God sets before us the classic choice, offering us blessing if we follow God's commandments and curses if we do not. God tells us to be a holy (*kadosh*) nation in everything we do: in our eating practices, in how we treat our bodies, in how we build our society, in how we preserve our natural resources. The *parashah* ends with a review of the pilgrimage festivals (Passover, Shavuot and Sukkot), describing the mitzvah to journey to the central place of worship.

OUR ToRAH TEXT: DEUTERoNOMY 15:8

In this *sidrah*, we find another anchor for a well known mitzvah, offering *tzedakah*.

כִּי־פָתֹחַ תִּפְתַּח אֶת־יָדְךָ לוֹ וְהַעֲבֵט תַּעֲבִיטֶנּוּ
דֵּי מַחְסֹרוֹ אֲשֶׁר יֶחְסַר לוֹ:

כי פתח תפתח את ידך והעבט תעביטנו
די מחסרו אשר יחסר לו

For you must open your hand to a person in need and lend them enough for their needs.

RASHI'S COMMENTARY

Rashi has SO much to say on this verse!

- **open**—The Hebrew text of our verse reads *fatach tiftach*—literally "Open! You will open…" The Torah sometimes doubles its verbs like this for emphasis, not just "you will open" but "you must open." Rashi says not only must you open your hand but you must do it multiple times!

- **lend**—if they won't accept a gift, offer a loan instead

- **their needs**—even if they need a horse to ride on and a person to run before them. Rashi explains that, while we do not need to make someone rich, we are expected to offer as much as we are capable of doing safely.

Reflection Question: What values do you think Rashi is trying to uphold or communicate through his commentary?

EXPLORING OUR ToRAH TEXT

Rabbi Moses ben Maimon, also known as Maimonides, was one of the greatest Jewish scholars of all time. He spent much of his time writing books that help Jews apply the laws and teaching of the Torah to the way they live and treat other people. He identified eight different ways, or levels, of following this commandment.

These are the eight rungs of Maimonides' ladder of tzedakah. See if you can put them in order (1 = lowest, 8 = highest).

_____ One who gives money directly to the person in need before the person has to ask.

_____ One who gives doesn't know who will receive the money, and the person who receives the money doesn't know who has given it.

_____ One who gives directly to the poor person but gives less than they should, even though the tzedakah is given cheerfully.

_____ One who gives knows who will get the money, but the person who receives the tzedakah doesn't know who gave it.

_____ One who helps a person help themself by entering into a partnership or helping that person find a job.

_____ One who gives tzedakah with a scowl. No matter how it is given, giving tzedakah is a mitzvah.

_____ One who gives money directly to the person in need after being asked.

_____ One who gives tzedakah without knowing who will receive it, while the person who receives the tzedakah knows who has given it.

Reflection Question: Maimonides' ladder begins at rung one. Is there a rung zero? What does it say that Maimonides does not include rung zero in his ladder?

ToRAH EXPERIENCE

Using the case below, stage a courtroom in the classroom to adjudicate the case. You'll need a judge, lawyers for both sides and a jury. If you have a big class, you might consider having witnesses or experts present as well.

The New York City Transit Authority issued a regulation that banned begging and panhandling in New York City subways. It did, however, allow organized charities to solicit funds. A beggar named Young challenged the legality of this regulation, and the case was heard before the New York State Supreme Court.

MITZVAH OF THE WEEK: צְדָקָה *TZEDAKAH*

The origins of a word can teach us a lot about their meaning. The English word that is closest to *tzedakah* is "justice," but when we talk about giving money to help those who are in need, we often use the words "charity" and "philanthropy." Using the chart below and dictionaries as needed, try to find the difference in their meanings.

Word	Language of Origin	Root Words	Definition
tzedakah	Hebrew	tzedek (justice, righteousness)	
charity	Latin	caritas (love, fondness)	
philanthropy	Greek	phila (love) + anthropos (people)	

Based on their root meanings, what is the difference between the Jewish mitzvah of giving *tzedakah* and the practice of giving charity or philanthropy?

ḤEVRUTA LEARNING

We talk about "giving" money to charity or to people that need it. The word "giving" implies that it is a gift, an option, a nice thing to do. Performing the mitzvah of tzedakah, though, is not simply a gift. It is an obligation that each of us carries, and it makes the world a more just, a more righteous place. Is "giving" the best action verb to go with *tzedakah*? With your *ḥevruta* partner, discuss options for other, perhaps better, verbs. Try out words like *give, offer, donate, perform, provide, contribute*. Which work works best, and why?

צְדָקָה *TZEDAKAH* EXPERIENCE

When we discuss *tzedakah*, we often think of it in the form of money. However, that is only one form that *tzedakah* can take. As a class, create a list of organizations in your area that serve the goal of *tzedakah* by making the community a better place. Research those organizations to learn how you can support their work beyond, or in addition to, sending money.

Make a plan for how you can get involved.

צְדָקָה *TZEDAKAH* RESOURCES

In the United States, we talk about "not for profit" organizations. Elsewhere they speak about NGOs (non-governmental organizations). They are the same. They are groups that are designed to improve situations. Some of these are funded by families or corporations; most of them are looking for funds. Donating to them is a form of *tzedakah*. Here are a few of our favorites that haven't yet fit into this book.

- One Laptop per Child—https://laptop.org/
- Wounded Warrior Project—http://www.woundedwarriorproject.org/
- Repair the World—http://werepair.org/

שֹׁפְטִים SHOFTiM

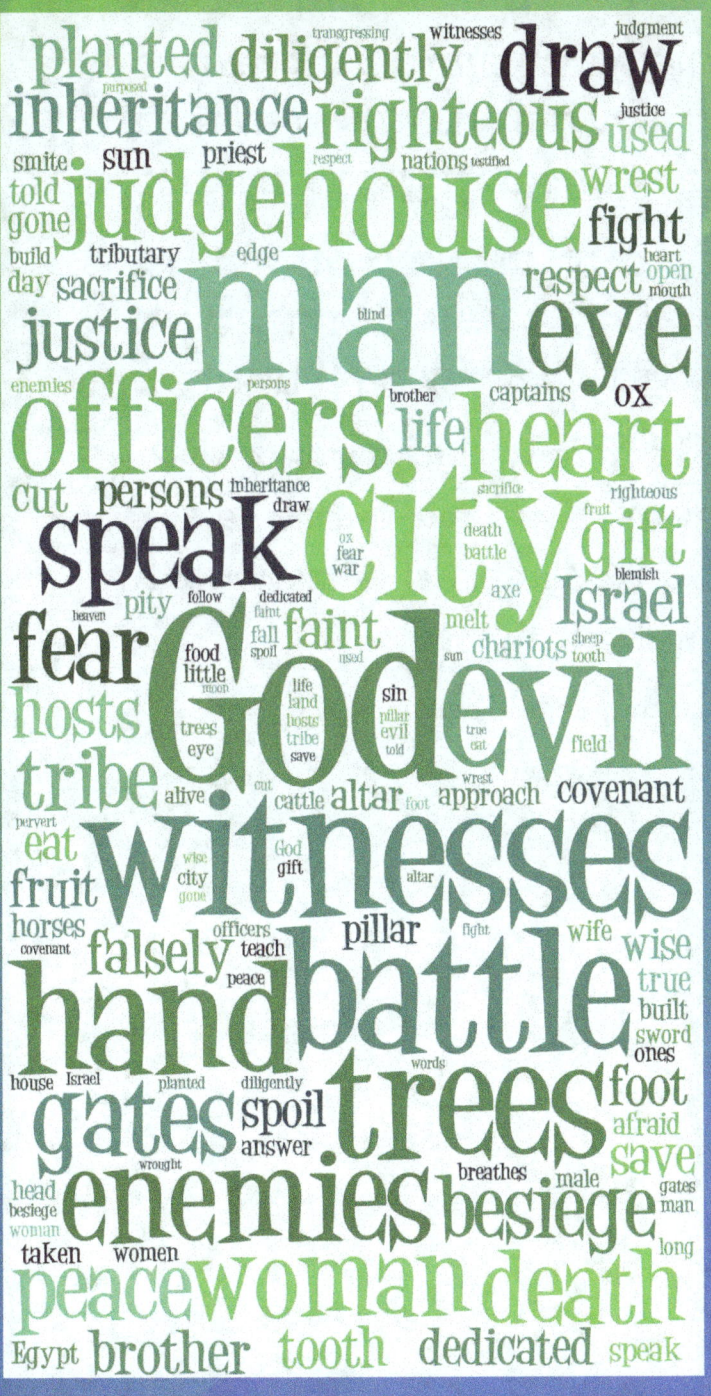

OVERVIEW: DEUTERONOMY 16:18–21:9

More laws are reviewed: the appointment of judges, laws against worshiping idols, laws concerning the high court, king, priests and Levites, criminal laws and the laws of warfare.

OUR ToRAH TEXT: DEUTERoNOMY 20:19

In this *sidrah* we find some Jewish rules of war. Here, one rule of war has big ecological ramifications.

כִּי־תָצוּר אֶל־עִיר יָמִים רַבִּים לְהִלָּחֵם עָלֶיהָ לְתָפְשָׂהּ
לֹא־תַשְׁחִית אֶת־עֵצָהּ לִנְדֹּחַ עָלָיו גַּרְזֶן כִּי מִמֶּנּוּ תֹאכֵל
כִּי הָאָדָם עֵץ הַשָּׂדֶה לָבֹא מִפָּנֶיךָ בַּמָּצוֹר:

כי תצור אל עיר ימים רבים להלחם עליה לתפשה
לא תשחית את עצה לנדח עליו גרזן כי ממנו תאכל
כי האדם עץ השדה לבא מפניך במצור

When you besiege a city for a long time, making war against it in order to capture it, you shall not destroy the trees by wielding an ax against them, for you may eat of them. You should not cut them down.

Are the trees in the field people that they should be attacked by you?

RASHI'S COMMENTARY

Our commentators get into the weeds arguing whether the last part of the verse should be a statement or a question, but really, they are asking where we separate the sentences within the verse. Unlike English, biblical Hebrew does not have punctuation! Instead, we have to come to a mutual understanding.

Rashi thinks it is a rhetorical question as written above, while Nachmanides, Ibn Ezra, and Bekhor Shor see it as a statement: "You should not cut them down because the trees of the field are human," meaning that trees have similar value to human life.

Compare and contrast these two translations of the text.

CHEVRUTA LEARNING

A Chinese proverb teaches that the best time to plant a tree is 20 years ago. The second best time is today. A famous Jewish story teaches this as well:

> One day, Honi was walking along the road when he saw a certain man planting a carob tree. Honi said to him: "How many years will it take for this tree to bear fruit?" The man replied: "It will not produce fruit until seventy years have passed." Honi said to him: "Do you really expect to live long enough to eat the fruit of this tree?" The old man said to Honi: "I found a world full of carob trees. Just as my ancestors planted for me, I too am planting for my descendants." (Taanit 23a)

Reflection Question: Have you ever planted a tree, or a plant, or a flower? If so, how did it feel to watch it grow?

Background History of Sources

- **The Tanakh**. Also known as the Jewish or Hebrew Bible, the Tanakh is made up of three parts: the Torah, the Prophets (*Nivi'im* in Hebrew) and the Writings (*Ketuvim*). The word Tanakh is just an acronym of the first letters of these three parts! The Tanakh contains the earliest forms of Jewish laws, Jewish teachings, and Jewish stories.

- **The Mishnah** is the first part of the Talmud. It was written by a group of scholars called the Rabbis who lived between 200 B.C.E. and 200 C.E. The Mishnah is divided into six orders, and there are many books in each of these orders. The Mishnah groups laws found in the Bible and adds and adapts laws for later societies. In the Mishnah, almost every word is part of a simple statement of the rule and its application.

- **The Gemara** is the second part of the Talmud. Between 200 and 500 C.E. Additional Rabbis added their own comments to the Mishnah. This updating and expansion of the Mishnah again helped to adapt the laws to the latest changes and problems in society. Unlike the Mishnah, which is basically a direct law code, the Gemara is filled with dialogue, stories and other interesting tangents. The Talmud (Mishnah and Gemara together) forms the heart of the Jewish legal process.

EXPLORING OUR ToRAH TEXT

Our Torah verse travels through Jewish history and grows into a completely different set of practices. Look at how it expands. Here are five Jewish sources that restate or expand on our verse's teaching.

Read all five, then number them in the order in which you think they were written. The descriptions on the following page will help you.

_____ **Text A. Kiddushin 32a**: Whoever breaks vessels, or tears garments, or destroys a building, or clogs up a well, or does away with food in a destructive manner violates the negative mitzvah of bal tash-hit (do not waste).

_____ **Text B. Mishneh Torah, Mourning 14:24**: One should be trained not to be destructive. When you bury a person do not waste garments by burying them in the grave. It is better to give them to the poor than to cast them to worms and moths. Anyone who buries the dead in an expensive garment violates the negative mitzvah of bal tash'hit.

_____ **Text C. Shevi'ith 4:10**: How much fruit should an olive tree produce so that it may be considered a fruit-bearing tree and should not be cut down (lo tash'hit)? Rabbi Simeon ben Gamaliel taught a rova (1 rova = 33.6 cubic inches).

_____ **Text D. Deuteronomy 20:19–20**: When you besiege a city for a long time, making war against it in order to capture it, you shall not destroy (lo tash'hit) the trees by wielding an ax against them, for you may eat of them. You should not cut them down. Are the trees in the field people that they should be besieged by you?

_____ **Text E. Shulhan Arukh, Laws of Body and Soul, Section 14**: It is forbidden to destroy anything that can be useful to people.

As a class, create a text timeline using the texts above. Rewrite each quote, in the original and in your own words, and hang them along the wall in order, along with illustrations of your understanding of the text on each poster.

- **_The Codes_**. As the times changed people had questions about how the laws of the Talmud should be applied in their day and in their situation. They ran into two problems. First, as society continued to change and evolve, new problems arose that called for new interpretations. Second, it was often difficult to find a particular law in the Talmud. The solution came with the creation of the Codes. The Codes were books that organized the law by subject and included all the rules that had been added to deal with new situations. While there are many Codes of Jewish law, the two most famous are the Mishneh Torah, which was written by Maimonides (Moses ben Maimon) in the twelfth century, and the Shulhan Arukh, which was written in the sixteenth century by Joseph Caro.

- **_The Responsa_**. Meanwhile, the Jewish legal process didn't stop with the Codes. People still faced situations that demanded interpretations of the law. When a local rabbi felt unable to work out a correct answer he would draft a letter to a leading scholar. These letters and their answers were collected as volumes of Responsa. These, too, became part of the literature Jews consult to find the right application of the Torah to their situation.

MITZVAH OF THE WEEK: בַּל תַּשְׁחִית *BAL TASH'HIT*

Based on the five sources in the activity above, create a class definition of this *mitzvah*.

_____

_____

_____

_____

EXPERIENCING בַּל תַּשְׁחִית *BAL TASH'HIT*—A *SH'ELAH*

The following letter was sent by the board of a synagogue to a famous scholar. The congregation whose board composed the letter was faced with a Jewish legal question they did not know how to answer. To find a solution they followed an ancient Jewish practice of consulting a respected, wise Jewish scholar.

There is a whole body of Jewish literature made up of letters requesting legal advice and answers received. These are called responsa. Each responsum is made up of two parts: the *sh'elah* (the request) and the *t'shuvah* (the answer).

Dear Rabbi:

We seek your counsel in helping this congregation resolve a question of great moral and practical significance.

Like many congregations, our synagogue has a contract with a caterer who has the exclusive right to provide food for functions in our social hall. For this privilege Mr. Reuben pays an annual fee and donates a fixed percentage of his income to the congregation.

He is also expected to provide certain free food services to the congregation. He is a good man, and the relationship is indeed beneficial to the community.

In our community there is a shelter that houses and feeds those without homes. Our congregation makes regular donations to this shelter, and some of the members volunteer time there. Recently the shelter requested that we turn over food that is left over after weddings and b'nai mitzvah celebrations. Normally this food is thrown out, since state health codes forbid it being served again.

Based on this request, our board enacted a congregational policy that all leftover foods would indeed be donated to the shelter. When this policy was presented to our caterer, he refused to follow it. He explained that it would cost him substantial time and money to make this food available. Most of our board is also in business and, understanding the caterer's position, reversed the policy.

When our rabbi learned of the change, he instructed the board that there is a principle of Jewish law called bal tash'hit that forbids Jews to waste any valuable resource. He said that it was our obligation to see to it that this food was not destroyed. While his position seems correct morally, it seems unfair to ask either the congregation or the caterer to bear the expense of making this food available.

Our rabbi suggested that we write to you and seek your insight. Thank you.

When a rabbi writes a *t'shuvah* (response) to a legal problem, they don't just give their own opinions. Writing a *halakhic* response is a research project. A rabbi checks all previous sources and finds the cases and laws that apply.

Write your own *t'shuvah* (response) to this letter.

בַּל תַּשְׁחִית *BAL TASH'HiT* RESOURCES

Here are a few of many foundations that work on not wasting the environment.

- Audubon Society—http://www.audubon.org/
- Sea Save—http://seasave.org/
- Wood's Hole Oceanographic Institute—http://www.whoi.edu/

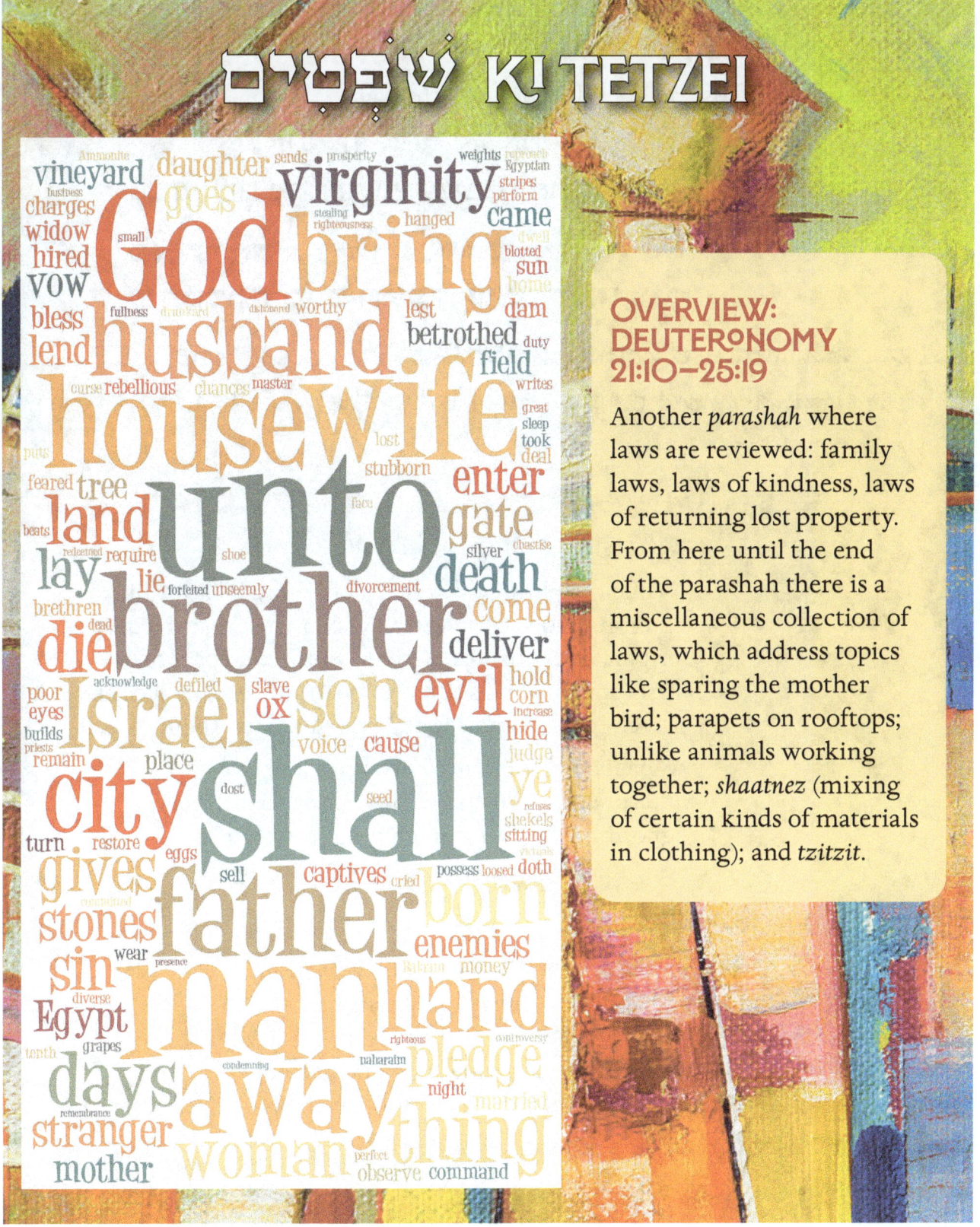

OVERVIEW: DEUTERONOMY 21:10–25:19

Another *parashah* where laws are reviewed: family laws, laws of kindness, laws of returning lost property. From here until the end of the parashah there is a miscellaneous collection of laws, which address topics like sparing the mother bird; parapets on rooftops; unlike animals working together; *shaatnez* (mixing of certain kinds of materials in clothing); and *tzitzit*.

OUR ToRAH TEXT: DEUTERoNOMY 22:1

All Jewish laws of lost and found come from this verse.

לֹא־תִרְאֶה אֶת־שׁוֹר אָחִיךָ אוֹ אֶת־שֵׂיוּ נִדָּחִים
וְהִתְעַלַּמְתָּ מֵהֶם הָשֵׁב תְּשִׁיבֵם לְאָחִיךָ :

לא תראה את שׁור אזיך או את שׂיו נדזים
והתעלבמת מהם השׁב תשׁיבם לאזיך

You shall not see your neighbor's ox or sheep gone astray and ignore it. You must bring them back to your neighbor.

RASHI'S COMMENTARY

While the phrase "you may not ignore it" is a valid interpretation of the verse, Rashi focuses on the deeper, original meaning. In Hebrew, the second part of the first sentence reads וְהִתְעַלַּמְתָּ מֵהֶם *v'hitalamta meihem*, which means "and conceal yourself from them".

What is the difference between these two interpretations? What is the difference between ignoring something and hiding oneself from it?

ToRAH EXPERIENCE

Almost every synagogue, every school, every library, even every hotel has a Lost and Found, a collection of forgotten and misplaced items. Does having a Lost and Found fulfill the *mitzvah* of our Torah verse? If you find something and present it to the Lost and Found, have you fulfilled your responsibility?

Split the class into groups and debate these questions.

EXPLORING OUR ToRAH TEXT

These two pieces of Mishnah expand our verse by stating when a finder must try to return a lost object and when the lost object may be kept.

Bava Metzia 2:1

If a person finds a lost object, when may the finder keep the object, and when must the found object be publicly advertised?

The following objects belong to the finder:

- scattered fruit
- scattered money
- small sheaves of grain (on a public street)
- cakes of figs
- loaves of bakers' bread
- strings of fish
- pieces of meat
- bundles of combed flax
- strips of purple wool

These belong to the finder, according to Rabbi Meir.

Rabbi Judah says, "Everything that has personal markings or changes must be publicly advertised."

"Explain!"

"For example, if one finds a bundle of figs with a potsherd in it or a loaf with a coin in it." Rabbi Shimon ben Elazar says, "All brand-new items with no identification or sign of use need not be advertised."

Exploring our Torah Text, continued on page 42

Bava Metzia 2:2

The following must be advertised as found by the finder.

- fruit in a container or just an empty container
- money in a bag or just an empty bag
- a pile of fruit
- a pile of money
- three coins on top of each other
- small sheaves of grain in a private area
- homemade loaves of bread

These must be advertised.

Restate the basic principles in your own words.

A finder may keep a lost object when _____

_____

A finder must try to return a lost object when _____

_____

Make posters that remind students to bring found objects to the school office. Posters should include some Jewish text explanation of why it is important to return found items.

Reflection Question: Why are laws about lost and found important?

MITZVAH OF THE WEEK: RETURNING LOST OBJECTS

It is a *mitzvah* to return lost property to its owner. One is obligated to return lost property, even if it is worth as little as a penny. The finder is obligated to care for the found article until it is claimed by its rightful owner. If it is something that may deteriorate or die, such as fresh food or an ill animal, they may sell it and hold the money for the owner. In the interim, the finder is required to make the public aware of their finding. This could take the form of announcements or posting notices.

The original owner may claim the lost article only if they can properly identify it by a unique characteristic or a definitive description of the object, such as size, color or some kind of imperfection. This *mitzvah* applies even to real property. For example, if one sees that an onrushing river is about to demolish a home or field, one must work intensely to put up a dam in order to prevent a disaster.

HEVRUTA LEARNING

As part of their conversations about lost property, the rabbis identify an emotion called *ye'ush*. *Ye'ush* means "despair." In this case, it means that one has given up on ever recovering a lost item. The rabbis say that when someone experiences *ye'ush*, they let go of their claim on that object. If someone then finds it, they can keep it. If a finder can reasonably assume that the original owner would have experienced *ye'ush* already, they can keep it from the moment they find it.

Share with your partner a story of when you have experienced *ye'ush* for a lost object.

EXPERIENCING LOST AND FOUND

Use your understanding of the two *mishnayot* above to explain what should be done with each of these found objects. Put a K in front of every item you can keep. Put an A in front of every item you must advertise. Circle every case in which you think the Mishnah's categories should be reconsidered.

_____ A) A wallet with $5 and no identification found on the floor of a classroom with eighteen students and one teacher.

_____ B) A wallet with $5 and no identification found on the floor of a cafeteria of a company with 250 employees.

_____ C) A wallet with $5 and no identification found in a local sports stadium.

_____ D) A bag of groceries left on a bus stop bench.

_____ E) Two bleachers tickets to a World Series baseball game.

_____ F) A six-pack of diet cola left on a mailbox.

_____ G) A briefcase left in a taxi or Uber.

_____ H) A briefcase left in a synagogue boardroom.

_____ I) A bag with six USB drives, all unopened.

_____ J) A homemade green sweater with the name Buzz woven into the sleeve.

_____ K) A green polo sweater (size medium).

_____ L) A lottery ticket.

_____ M) Tickets 137 through 145 to the Beth El Congregation dinner with the name Heller written on the back of the first ticket.

_____ N) A video game left in a gaming console that you bought secondhand.

_____ O) Three sheets of brand-new plywood sitting in a vacant lot.

_____ P) An empty gym bag left in the lobby of an apartment building.

_____ Q) An empty gym bag left by a basketball court in a public park.

_____ R) $25 in quarters spilled in the alley.

_____ S) A briefcase with $5,000 left behind under a park bench.

_____ T) A bundle of figs and a potsherd left in the middle of a shopping center.

_____ U) A pair of expensive skis (which probably fell off a car roof) sitting by the side of the road. On each is the mark H.I. Stu.

_____ V) A brand new iPhone, still in the box, left on the railing of a freeway overpass.

_____ W) A case of baseball bats left in an alley.

_____ X) A dog found at the back door without any identification tags.

_____ Y) A rough draft of an essay for a competition with the initials D.M.

_____ Z) A golf ball with "Love, Joanne" imprinted in gold letters, found near a public golf course.

Adapted from Rabbi Morley Feinstein, *The Jewish Law Review*

LOST AND FOUND RESOURCES

Finding and redeeming is a kind of lost and found. Here are a few of many rescue foundations.

- Rescue Foundation—http://www.rescuefoundation.net/
- Lost Dog and Cat Rescue Foundation—http://www.lostdogandcatrescue.org/
- Search Dog Foundation—http://www.searchdogfoundation.org/

כִּי־תָבוֹא KI TAVO

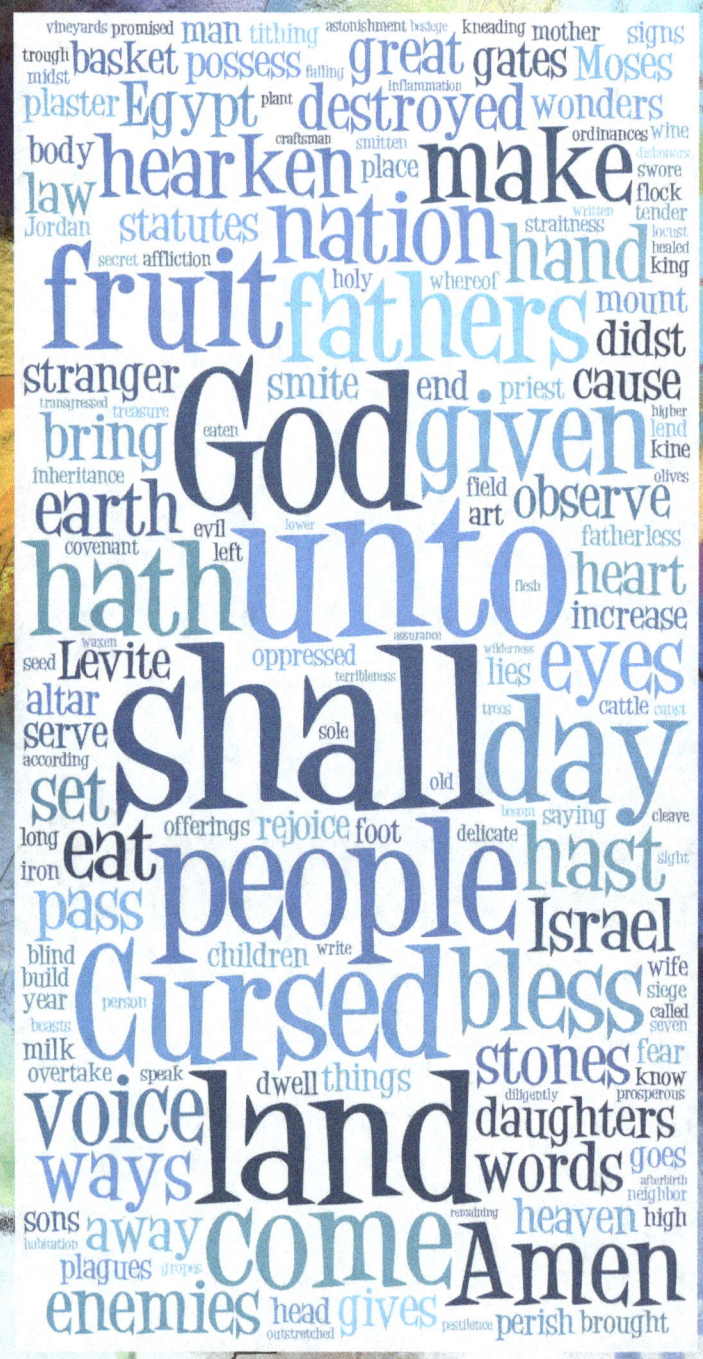

vineyards promised man tithing astonishment besiege kneading mother signs trough basket possess falling great gates Moses midst plaster Egypt plant destroyed wonders wine body craftsman inflammation smitten ordinances distances hearken place make swore law written flock Jordan statutes nation straitness tender locust secret affliction holy whereof hand healed king fruit fathers mount didst stranger smite end priest cause higher transgressed treasure eaten lend kine bring God given olives inheritance field observe earth evil lower art fatherless covenant left flesh heart hath unto increase waxen assurance seed Levite oppressed wilderness lies eyes altar terribleness cattle canst serve shall sole day trees according old set bosom saying cleave long eat offerings rejoice foot delicate hast iron people sight blind children write Israel build wife year person siege called milk seven beasts Cursed bless stones fear overtake speak dwell things diligently prosperous know voice land daughters ways words goes afterbirth neighbor sons away come heaven high habitation remaining plagues droves enemies head gives pestilence perish brought

OVERVIEW: DEUTERONOMY 26:1–29:8

This portion acknowledges God as the giver of all, to whom we celebrate with first fruits and other sacrifices. We review the laws of first fruits and tithes, then we receive descriptions of three tithes: to the Levites, to the owner of Jerusalem, and to the poor and dependent. Finally, we learn how to cross the Jordan River and that we must build an altar immediately after crossing.

OUR ToRAH TEXT: DEUTERoNOMY 28:9

Having retaught most of the laws, Moses launches into his big sermon.

יְקִימְךָ יי לוֹ לְעַם קָדוֹשׁ כַּאֲשֶׁר נִשְׁבַּע־לָךְ
כִּי תִשְׁמֹר אֶת־מִצְוֹת יי אֱלֹהֶיךָ וְהָלַכְתָּ בִּדְרָכָיו:

יקימך יהוה לו לעם קדוש כאשר נשבע לך
כי תשמר את מצות יהוה אלהיך והכלת בדרכיו

The Eternal will establish you as a holy people to God, as God has promised to do, if you will keep the commandments of the Eternal your God and walk in God's ways.

RASHI'S COMMENTARY

Rashi does not comment on our verse, but Ibn Ezra does. He offers a clear cut understanding of what it means to be a holy people. According to Ibn Ezra, we are made holy when we observe and perform God's *mitzvot*. Based on this description, how do you think Ibn Ezra understands holiness? Is it innate, within us, as an element of our beliefs or our ancestry? Or is it based solely on our actions? Or is it something else entirely?

ToRAH EXPERIENCE

According to the Torah, all people are created in God's image. Many people, including most Jewish, believe that God is incorporeal (a fancy word that means having no physical body). If God has no body, then how do we walk in God's ways?

Many people, including Ibn Ezra, understand this as a metaphor. How might we fulfill the metaphor? What actions do we need to take, what values do we need to uphold, to "walk in God's ways"?

EXPLORING OUR ToRAH TEXT

The rabbis of the Talmud asked themselves the same question: how do we walk in God's ways? They recorded their answer in the Talmud:

> Just as God clothes the naked, so should you also clothe the naked, for it is written, "The Eternal, the God, made for Adam and for his wife coats of skin, and clothed them." *(Genesis 3:21)*

> The Holy One visited the sick, so should you also visit the sick, for it is written, "The Eternal appeared to Abraham after his circumcision by the oaks of Mamre." *(Genesis 18:1)*

> The Holy One comforted mourners, so should you also comfort mourners, for it is written, "And it came to pass after the death of Abraham that God blessed Isaac, his son." *(Genesis 25:11)*

> The Holy One buried the dead, so should you also bury the dead, for it is written, "And God buried Moses in the valley." *(Deuteronomy 34:6) (Sotah 14a:4)*

Based on this passage, where do the rabbis turn to learn more about the ways of God?

Where do you look to find positive examples in your life? Who are your role models? How do you walk in their ways?

HEVRUTA LEARNING

Our verse focuses on walking in God's ways or God's roads or God's paths. The Hebrew word is דֶּרֶךְ *derekh*. Curiously, the rabbis also spend a lot of time talking about a different kind of *derekh*, something called דֶּרֶךְ אֶרֶץ *derekh eretz*. Literally, this means the "way of the world," but colloquially we might call this the way of doing things, common behavior. These two may seem disconnected, but the following passage connects them:

> Rabbi Elazar ben Azaryah says: "If there is no Torah, there is no *derekh eretz*. If there is no *derekh eretz*, there is no Torah. *(Pirkei Avot 3:17)*

Discuss with your *hevruta* what you think Rabbi Elazar means here.

MITZVAH OF THE WEEK: וְהָלַכְתָּ בִּדְרָכָיו
V'HALAKHTA B'DRAKHAV WALKING AFTER GOD

From our Torah text, we learn the mitzvah to emulate God's righteous ways. Some of these character traits include: compassion, kindness and graciousness towards others; forgiveness for iniquity; honesty, humility and tolerance *(Sefer ha-Hinukh)*.

EXPERIENCING וְהָלַכְתָּ בִּדְרָכָיו V'HALAKHTA B'DRAKHAV

Look up these two passages in the Torah. How do they expand our understanding of this mitzvah?

Genesis 1:27 _____

Exodus 34:6 _____

List ten things you can do to fulfill this mitzvah.

1. _____
2. _____
3. _____
4. _____
5. _____
6. _____
7. _____
8. _____
9. _____
10. _____

וְהָלַכְתָּ בִּדְרָכָיו V'HALAKHTA B'DRAKHAV RESOURCES

Walks, rides and runs are ways of raising money, particularly to cure diseases. Here are some URLs of foundations about walking.

- America Walks—https://americawalks.org/
- Wheel to Walk Foundation—http://www.wheeltowalk.com/
- Walk Strong Foundation—http://www.walkstrongfoundation.org/

נִצָּבִים NiTZAVIM

OVERVIEW: DEUTERONOMY 29:9–30:20

Moses speaks to all Israelites who have entered and will enter into the covenant. He explains that God does not want to punish the Families-of-Israel; if we seek God, God will show mercy. Moses explains that God's commandments are not hard and distant but practical to follow and very close to us.

OUR ToRAH TEXT: DEUTERoNOMY 30:19

Moses' life is almost over. He is finishing up his State of the Wilderness speech. Our verse is one of the great sound bites from that address.

הַעִדֹתִי בָכֶם הַיּוֹם אֶת־הַשָּׁמַיִם וְאֶת־הָאָרֶץ הַחַיִּים וְהַמָּוֶת נָתַתִּי לְפָנֶיךָ הַבְּרָכָה וְהַקְּלָלָה וּבָחַרְתָּ בַּחַיִּים לְמַעַן תִּחְיֶה אַתָּה וְזַרְעֶךָ:

הָעִדֹתִי בכם היום את השמים ואת ארץ הזיים והמות נתתי לפניך ברכה והקללה ובחרת בזיים למען תזיה אתה וזרעך

I call heaven and earth to bear witness for you today, that I have given you a choice, that I have placed before you – life, the blessing, and death, the curse – choose life that you will live, you and your descendants after you.

RASHI'S CoMMENTARY

Several of our commentators, Rashi included, make note of the perceived permanence of heaven and earth. The sun rises each day and sets each night. It is constant, and we can rely on it. We humans, however, are not permanent, not are we constant. The universe follows natural law, but we humans get to make decisions, choices that vary day to day, even moment to moment. According to Rashi, God encourages us to choose life, to choose blessings, just as consistently as the sun rises!

EXPLORING OUR ToRAH TEXT

The comedian Eddie Izzard has an old joke about a very easy decision. He imagines an authority figure offering you two choices: Cake, or Death! To quote Eddie, "Um, cake please!"

At first glance, it may seem like our Torah verse is offering a decision that is just as easy: Life and Blessing, or Death and Curse. Um, life please!

But life is rarely that easy. How exactly do we choose life? For that, we have to look at the very next verse:

By loving Adonai your God, heeding God's commands, and holding fast to God. For thereby you shall have life and shall long endure upon the soil that Adonai swore to your ancestors Abraham, Isaac, and Jacob, to give to them.

How else might we choose life?

ToRAH EXPERIENCE

Unlike the heavens and the earth, we have to make choices every day. Often this takes discipline, and it can require us to create healthy habits. Make a list of all the healthy habits that you do every day.

Now brainstorm some new healthy habits that you would like to incorporate into your daily activities. Choose one and make a plan for how to make it a habit.

MiTZVAH OF THE WEEK: פִּקּוּחַ נֶפֶשׁ *PIKU'AH NEFESH*

The Torah tells us to choose life. Sometimes, saving a person's life might require us to break a rule or a law. Judaism teaches that, in those situations, we should break the rule. We call this value *Pikuakh Nefesh*, saving a soul. Protecting a human life is a major Jewish obligation.

HEVRUTA LEARNING

Leviticus 18:5 says "You shall keep My laws and My rules, by the pursuit of which humans shall live: I am Adonai." The rabbis use this verse to value of *Pikuakh Nefesh*. Can you explain how? Work with your partner to see if you can come up with the answer.

_____

_____

_____

Answer: The rabbis of the Talmud point out that this verse says "humans shall **live**" by God's *mitzvot*. It does not say that we should **die** by them! Therefore, they teach, in just about every situation, if we have to choose between saving a person's life and following a Jewish law, we choose the life!

פְּקוּחַ נֶפֶשׁ *PIKU'AH NEFESH* EXPERIENCE:

The rabbis discuss several situations in which it is ok to break Jewish law in order to save a person's life, or even to help them heal. Read the following examples and discuss what you think the best course of action would be. Then decide if these are valid examples of *Pikuakh Nefesh*.

YES NO 1. It is Yom Kippur. Your little sister is a diabetic. You are concerned that her insulin level is out of balance and that her blood sugar level is dangerously low. She wants to continue the fast. You think she should eat. Should you insist that she eat?

YES NO 2. It is the seventh night of Hanukkah. Cynthia's whole family is due at the JCC to see a Hanukkah play. The family lights the candles and then prepares to leave. Cynthia's mom wants to blow out the candles because she is worried that there might be an accident if they burned with no one around. Cynthia's brother says that it is against Jewish law to blow out Hanukkah candles. Should the family blow the Hanukkah candles out?

YES NO 3. Larry does not keep kosher, but one day a bully in his school threatens to beat him up unless Larry eats a ham sandwich. The bully knows that Larry is Jewish and that Jews don't eat ham. Normally eating the sandwich wouldn't bother Larry. Should he eat it?

With a partner, create some of your own situations for other people to debate.

פְּקוּחַ נֶפֶשׁ *PIKU'AH NEFESH* RESOURCES

Transplants are the latest lifesaving frontier.

- Gift of Life—Bone Marrow Donation—http://www.giftoflife.org/default.aspx
- Gift Donor—Organ Donation—http://www.giftdonor.org/
- Save a Child's Heart—https://saveachildsheart.org/

sons Amorites Mishkans women men Sihon ETERNAL come years book called courage death spoken Assemble bore sworn destroyed corruptly honey God words teach break flowing wrought meeting gates devoured ears read wrote spoke come turned tent Joshua end tribes hands rebellious covenant strong stranger tzitzit release choose time taught face witness land old Moses presented astray children live fat pass surely Nun gave fear set die eiders Jordan swore milk cloud came approach fear end law fathers Levites law Moses aside meeting ones deal tent way sleep door priests went testify God know delivered alive ark learn bore foreign wrote earth rebellion officers Joshua feast Israel seed song years Levi day land befall place wise stiff cause eaten people broken sight hide song Israel witness heaven stood imagination little song possess rise kindled fail commanded hide speak work strong covenant long went swore inherit observe bring nations neck served hear evils day Og spoke good anger charge courage saying children seven Og good fathers appeared provoke Assemble words known despised forgotten commanded ark

OVERVIEW: DEUTERONOMY 31:1–31:30

Moses announces that Joshua will take over as his successor. He assures the people of Israel that God will still be with them. Moses gives Joshua public recognition that he has confidence in him as a leader. He then hands the law to the Levites to deposit in the aron.

OUR ToRAH TEXT: DEUTERoNOMY 31:19

Even though it may sound more poetic upon first reading, in this verse we find a special *mitzvah*.

וְעַתָּה כִּתְבוּ לָכֶם אֶת־הַשִּׁירָה הַזֹּאת
וְלַמְּדָהּ אֶת־בְּנֵי־יִשְׂרָאֵל שִׂימָהּ בְּפִיהֶם
לְמַעַן תִּהְיֶה־לִּי הַשִּׁירָה הַזֹּאת לְעֵד בִּבְנֵי־יִשְׂרָאֵל:

וְעַתה כתבו לכם את השירה הזֹאת
למדה את בני ישראל שימה בפיהם
למען תהיה לי השירה הזֹאת לעד בני ישראל

Now, write down this song and teach it to the people of Israel; put it in their mouths so that this song may be My witness among the people of Israel.

RASHI'S CoMMENTARY

We have already seen Ibn Ezra break the verse down into pieces and focus his commentary on specific parts. This time, he chose to comment on the verb "teach." What does it mean to teach something? From his comment, Ibn Ezra clearly thinks teaching is more than just making people memorize material. People can memorize just about anything, but is memorizing something the same as knowing it? Ibn Ezra says no. He comments that teaching means explaining the more difficult parts to people, helping them to understand Torah and apply it to their lives.

Reflection Question: Think of all the teachers you have had. Did any of them follow Ibn Ezra's advice? What did those teachers do differently than other teachers you have had?

EXPLORING OUR ToRAH TEXT

From this very verse, the rabbis made it a *mitzvah* for every Jew to write their very own Torah scroll, by hand! Even today, every *sefer Torah* is handwritten by a *sofer* (scribe), and they have to follow MANY rules!

Writing a *sefer Torah* is a long, hard process. It takes between nine months and a year of work to finish a Torah. It has to be written with the best permanent black ink, on parchment made from the skins of kosher animals. Instead of a pen or pencil, the *sofer* must use a quill or a reed. All of the separate parchments must be sewn together with sinews from kosher animals, and the *sofer* must use a thorn for a needle.

The *sofer* cannot write a single letter from memory. Instead, they must read it from a valid text, pronounce every word out loud, and only then copy it. Every letter and every word must be perfectly spaced. Every letter must be clearly drawn so that everyone can recognize it. In addition, the *sofer* has to add crowns to thirteen letters. The letters שׁ, עֲ, ג, ז, צ, and צ have three-stroke crowns, and the letters ב, ד, ק, ח, י, and ה have one-stroke crowns.

Here is a passage handwritten by a sofer. Add the crowns on your own.

תאזה הרישה תא מכל ובתכ התעו

To understand how hard it is to write a sefer Torah, look at this list of conditions that can make it un-kosher (and therefore unusable).

- If it was written on the skin of a non-kosher animal.
- If a clean skin was not made into parchment.
- If the parchment was not made specifically for a sefer Torah.
- If it was written on the wrong side of the parchment.
- If just one section was written on the wrong side of the parchment.
- If it was written without traced lines.

- If it was not written with indelible ink.
- If it was written in any language but Hebrew.
- If the *sofer* wrote the name of God without intention or focus (*kavannah*).
- If one letter was omitted.
- If one letter was added.
- If two letters touch.
- If one letter can be misread as another.
- If a letter can't be read.
- If one word looks like two.
- If two words look like one.
- If the *sofer* changed the form of any section.
- If it is not sewn together with the dry tendons of clean animals.

(Rambam, Mishneh Torah, Laws of the Sefer Torah, 10:1)

ḤEVRUTA LEARNING

Many people wonder why certain letters get special crowns on them when written in Torah. The rabbis wondered the same thing. In response, they tell this story:

> Rav Yehuda says that Rav says: When Moses ascended Mount Sinai, he found God sitting and tying crowns on the letters of the Torah. Moses said before God: Ruler of the Universe, who is preventing You from giving the Torah without these additions? God said to him: There is a man who is destined to be born after several generations, and Akiva ben Yosef is his name; he is destined to derive from each and every thorn of these crowns mounds upon mounds of wisdom. It is for his sake that the crowns must be added to the letters of the Torah. *(Menachot 29b:3)*

According to the story, Rabbi Akiva would be able to find deep meaning in something that others took for granted. Have you ever found meaning in something that other people overlooked? Talk about it with your partner.

ToRAH EXPERIENCE

One Hasidic rabbi took the laws for writing a sefer Torah and explained them this way:

> The many letters in the Torah represent the many souls of the Jewish people. If one single letter is left out of the Torah, it is unfit for use. If one single soul is left out of the union of the Jewish people, the Divine Presence will not join them. Like the letters, the souls must join together in a union.
>
> Then why is it forbidden for one letter to touch another? Because every soul must have its own unique relationship with its Creator. *(Rabbi Uri of Strelisk, from Tales of the Hasidim: Later Masters, Martin Buber, p. 147).*

MiTZVAH OF THE WEEK: WRiTiNG A ToRAH

As we have learned, it is a mitzvah for every Jew to write a Torah scroll for themselves. But we have also learned how hard it can be to write one. For example, the writing of a *sefer Torah* must be done in accordance with certain rules and specifications.

- It must be written by hand.
- It must be written on sheets of parchment made from the skin of a kosher animal.
- It must be written with special Hebrew lettering.

Reflection Question: Why do you think writing a Torah scroll has so many rules?

סֵפֶר תּוֹרָה *SEFER ToRAH* EXPERiENCE

As a class, write your very own *mezuzah* scrolls using the words of the *Shema* and the first line of *V'Ahavta*. If you need help, YouTube has videos that show scribes writing Torah scrolls and giving Hebrew calligraphy demonstrations. Be sure to use an actual Torah scroll, or another text with the exact way to write it in Torah letters, as an example

סֵפֶר תּוֹרָה *SEFER ToRAH* RESOURCES

The Torah uses music as a metaphor for itself. Here are some music foundations (including Jewish Rock Radio).

- Jewish Rock Radio—http://jewishrockradio.com/
- Fender Music Foundation—https://www.fenderplayfoundation.org/
- Save the Music Foundation—http://www.vh1savethemusic.com/
- Young Musicians Foundation—http://www.ymf.org/

הַאֲזִינוּ HA'AZINU

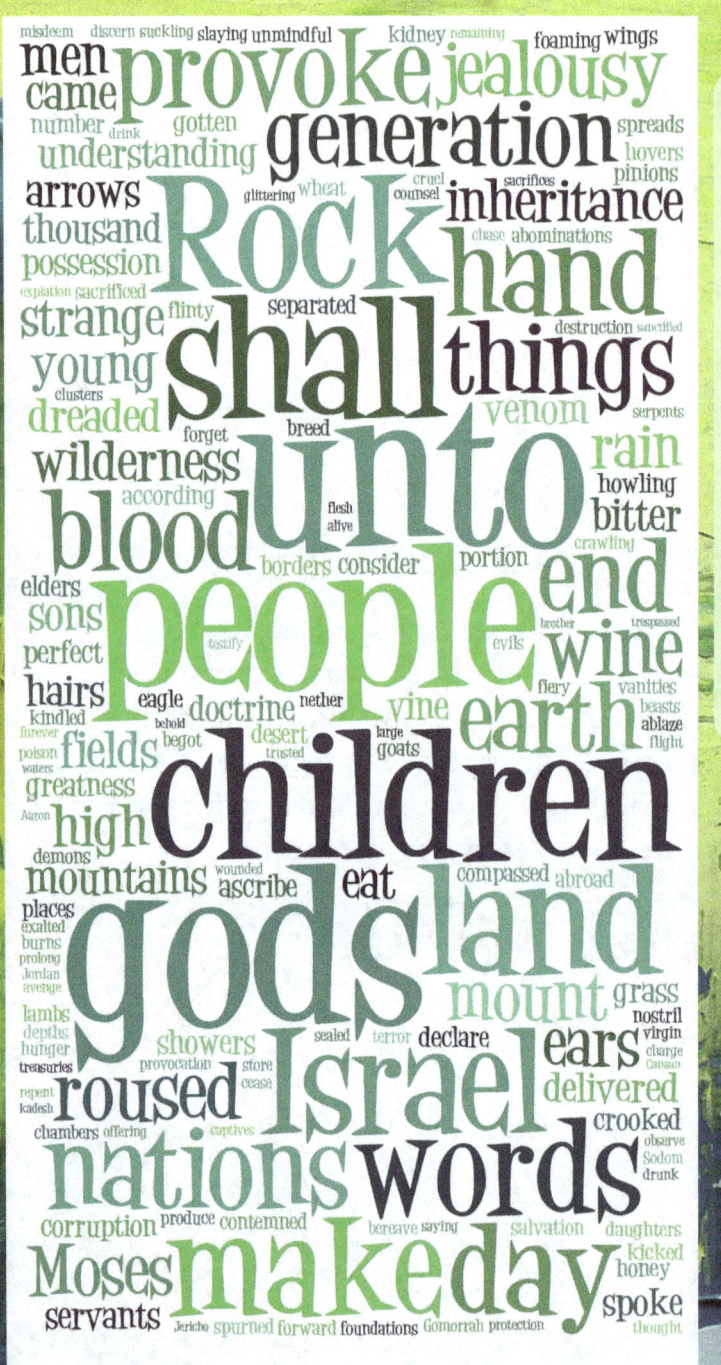

men came number drink gotten provoke jealousy foaming wings kidney remaining misdeem discern suckling slaying unmindful spreads understanding hovers generation pinions arrows glittering wheat cruel counsel inheritance sacrifices chase abominations thousand possession Rock hand sanctified expiation sacrificed strange flinty separated destruction young things shall clusters venom serpents dreaded forget breed flesh unto rain wilderness according howling blood borders consider portion bitter crawling elders testify people end wine sons perfect evils brother trespassed hairs eagle doctrine nether vine earth fiery vanities kindled behold begot desert large ablaze forever fields trusted goats flight poison waters children high greatness Aaron demons wounded compassed abroad mountains ascribe eat places exalted gods land burns prolong Jordan average mount grass lambs depths showers sealed terror declare ears nostril virgin hunger provocation store cease charge Canaan treasuries repent kadesh roused Israel delivered crooked chambers offering captives observe Sodom nations words drunk corruption produce contemned bereave saying salvation daughters Moses makeday honey kicked servants Jericho spurned forward foundations Gomorrah protection spoke thought

OVERVIEW: DEUTERONOMY 32:1–32:52

Moses sings the Song of Moses, a farewell to the people. He reviews history and takes from it the lessons to be learned and taught. He urges the people to take these words to heart. The *parashah* concludes with God telling Moses that he is to ascend Mount Nebo and to see the Promised Land from afar, and there he will die.

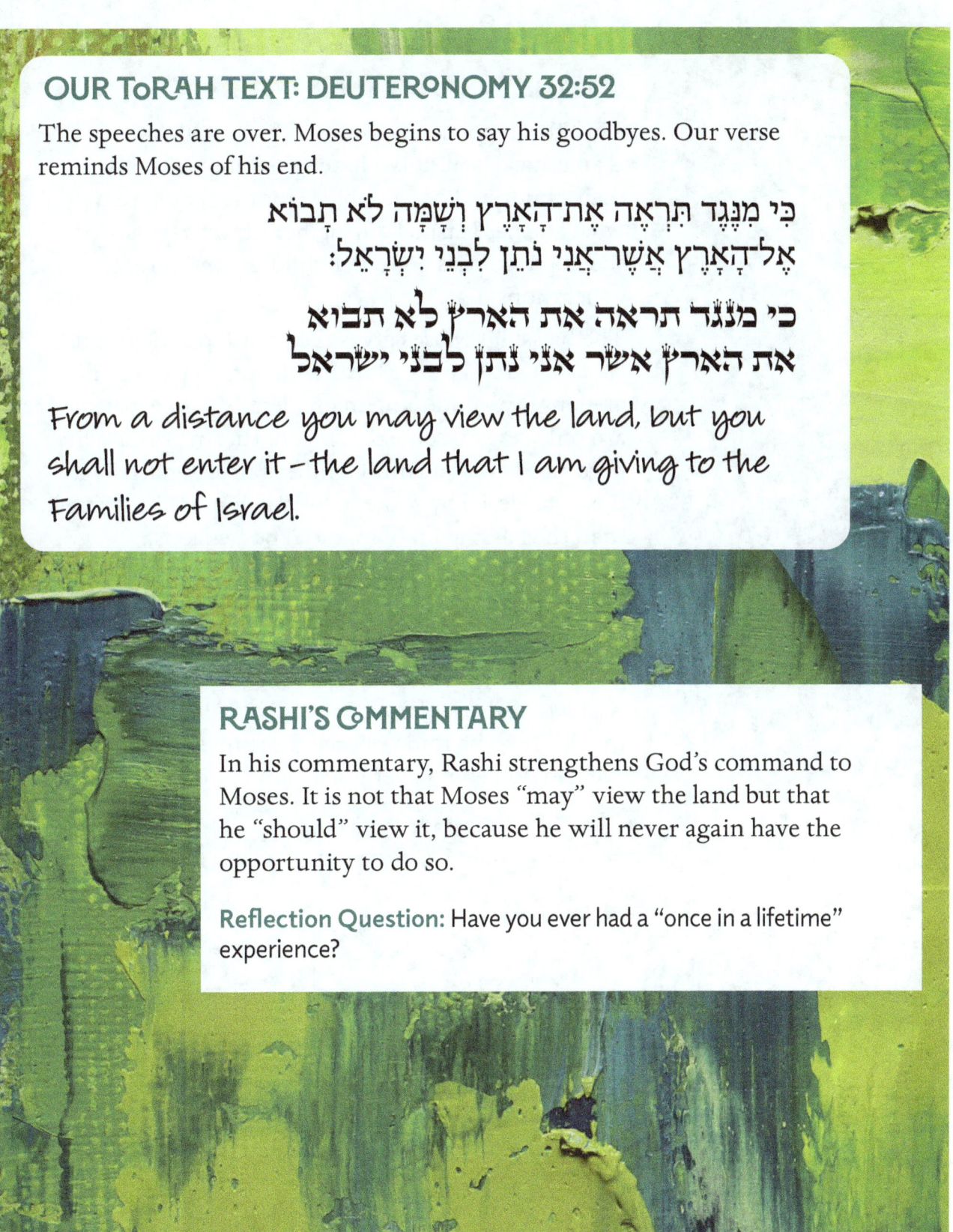

OUR ToRAH TEXT: DEUTERoNOMY 32:52

The speeches are over. Moses begins to say his goodbyes. Our verse reminds Moses of his end.

כִּי מִנֶּגֶד תִּרְאֶה אֶת־הָאָרֶץ וְשָׁמָּה לֹא תָבוֹא אֶל־הָאָרֶץ אֲשֶׁר־אֲנִי נֹתֵן לִבְנֵי יִשְׂרָאֵל:

כי מנגד תראה את הארץ לא תבוא את הארץ אשר אני נתן לבני ישראל

From a distance you may view the land, but you shall not enter it – the land that I am giving to the Families of Israel.

RASHI'S COMMENTARY

In his commentary, Rashi strengthens God's command to Moses. It is not that Moses "may" view the land but that he "should" view it, because he will never again have the opportunity to do so.

Reflection Question: Have you ever had a "once in a lifetime" experience?

EXPLORING OUR ToRAH TEXT

This Torah portion is Moses' ethical will. What is an ethical will? It is a letter a parent writes to their children. For example, a mother could share what she has learned during her life and the lessons she hopes to pass on to her children and future generations.

The blessings Moses gives the Jewish people in this *parashah* are like an ethical will. Some ethical wills are lengthy, containing many details, while others are only several sentences in length. An ethical will becomes part of a family's inheritance and heritage. It is considered by some to be much more important than the passing on of material possessions.

An ethical will can preserve a memory and, to some extent, shape the way that a person is remembered. That is one of the greatest challenges and the greatest dangers in writing an ethical will. We all wish we had done more in our lives. We have to fight the desire to be remembered for things that we wish we had done but never got around to doing.

HEVRUTA LEARNING

Here is an example of an ethical will. As you read it, ask yourself what it tells you about the author. Then answer the questions below with your partner.

The RAMBAN (Rabbi Moshe ben Nahman), a great scholar who lived in the thirteenth century in Spain, wrote the following to his children and students:

> Listen, my child, to the instruction of your father, and do not forget the teaching of your mother (Proverbs 1:8). Speak with kindness to all people always. This will save you from anger, the major cause of misdeed...Always be humble; regard every person as greater than yourself... Study Torah regularly so that you can fulfill its commandments. When you finish your studies, think carefully about what you have learned; try to translate your learning into action...
>
> When you pray, do not think about worldly matters, think only of God...Read this letter once a week, and be regular in carrying out its requirements. By doing so you will always walk in the path of God, and you will be worthy of all of the good that is due to the righteous.

Underline the values that the Ramban wants to pass on to his children. Why does he ask that the letter be read every week?

ToRAH EXPERIENCE

Many people get uncomfortable talking about death. It can be very hard to lose a loved one. It can be even more difficult thinking that each of us will someday die. Martin Buber, a 20th century Jewish scholar and philosopher, told a story about one rabbi's experience:

> Once, Rabbi Zusya came to his students with tears in his eyes. They asked him: "Rabbi, what's the matter?
>
> And he told them about a vision he had. "I learned the question that the angels will one day ask me about my life."
>
> The followers were puzzled. "Zusya, you are pious. You are scholarly and humble. You have helped so many of us. What question about your life could be so terrifying that you would be frightened to answer it?"
>
> Zusya replied: "I have learned that the angels will not ask me, 'Why weren't you more like Moses, leading your people out of slavery?' and that the angels will not ask me, 'Why weren't you more like Joshua, leading your people into the promised land?'"
>
> Zusya sighed. "They will say to me, 'Zusya, why weren't you more like Zusya?'"

What would it mean to be more like yourself, the real you? Use the space below to write your thoughts down in the form of a letter to yourself.

MITZVAH OF THE WEEK: OBEYING A LAST WILL AND TESTAMENT

It is a *mitzvah* to carry out the wishes of a person who has died. Thus it is a duty of the legal heirs to carry out the wishes of a person who wrote a will, and this is a duty the courts will enforce. However, the above rule is not always to be applied as a strict legal duty, and when the duty is merely a moral one, the court will not compel compliance with the wishes of the person who wrote the will's directions *(Shevut Ya'akov, vol. 1, no. 168)*.

MITZVAH EXPERIENCE

A living will or an advanced directive is an end-of-life document. It helps your relatives by telling them what you want to happen medically and by telling them what you don't want to happen to you. Download and fill out one of these forms at http://www.caringinfo.org

Bring a copy of the forms home. Have your parents fill them out. It is nothing that you will need now. But when you are an adult and your parents are old, it will save you from asking a lot of questions you don't want to ask.

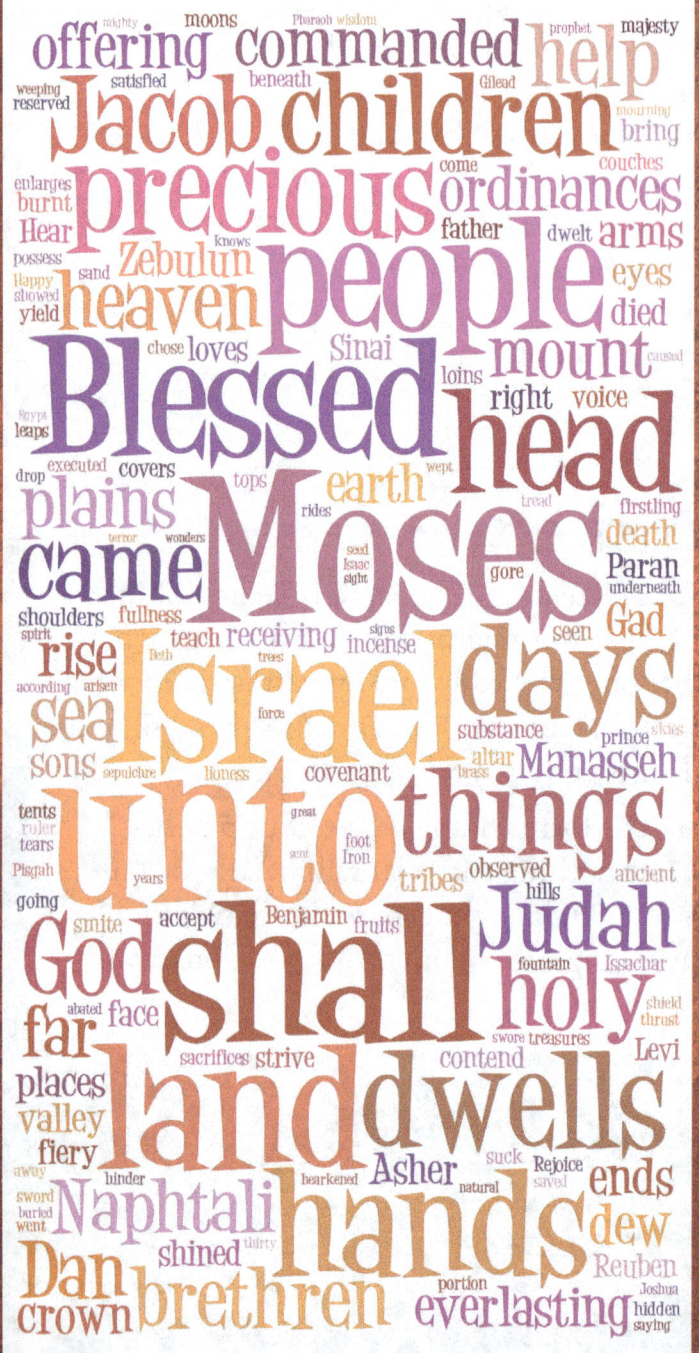

Moses blesses the Families-of-Israel tribe by tribe. Moses goes up to Mt. Nebo, has a chance to see the Promised Land one more time and dies. The people mourn him for thirty days. The Torah concludes with the verse "And there never again was a prophet in Israel like Moses, who knew God face to face" *(Deut. 34:10)*.

OUR ToRAH TEXT: DEUTERoNOMY 34:5

This is the end of the Torah. Not quite the last verse, but close to it. This is the moment when Moses dies.

וַיָּ֤מָת שָׁ֨ם מֹשֶׁ֥ה עֶֽבֶד־יי֙ בְּאֶ֣רֶץ מוֹאָ֔ב עַל־פִּ֖י יי׃

וימת שם משה עבד יהוה בארץ מואב על פי יהוה

Moses, the servant of the Eternal, died there in the land of Moav, by the command of God.

RASHI'S COMMENTARY

Another common name for Torah is the Five Books of Moses, based on the idea that Moses wrote it. But wait, Rashi asks, how did Moses write the Torah if it includes his death? Rashi answers that Moses wrote *most* of the Torah and that Joshua wrote the rest, from this very line onward. Other commentators think that Moses wrote the whole thing back on Sinai, and God dictated the whole thing!

EXPLORING OUR ToRAH TEXT

Many different scholars have translated Torah into many different languages. Every translation necessarily interprets the text a little differently. The following are three different translations/ interpretations. What do you make of them? Compare and contrast them with a partner.

JPS: by the word of God.

Literal: by the mouth of God.

Rashi: by a kiss from God.

ToRAH EXPERIENCE

This script comes from *Midrash P'tirat Moshe*, a collection of rabbinic stories about the way Moses died. It is not supposed to be a collection of facts about his death; rather, it is a way of talking about deeper truths. Our version is drawn from *Sefer ha-Aggadah*.

PROLOGUE

Narrator: AND THE ETERNAL SAID TO MOSES:

God: BEHOLD, IT IS GETTING CLOSE TO YOUR DAYS TO DIE *(Deuteronomy 31.14)*.

Narrator: Even Moses had to die. It says in the book of Job:

Bible: EVEN IF HE GOES UP TO HEAVEN, AND HIS HEAD REACHES UP TO THE CLOUDS, STILL HE SHALL DIE *(Job 20:6)*.

Narrator: This is the story of Moses, who went up to heaven, walked on clouds like an angel, spoke to God face to face and received the Torah from God's hand. Yet as soon as he reached the time for the natural end to his life, God told him:

God: BEHOLD, IT IS GETTING CLOSE TO YOUR DAYS TO DIE *(Deuteronomy 31.14)*.

SCENE 1: "I'LL HUFF, AND I'LL PUFF, AND I'LL PRAY YOUR GATES DOWN"

Narrator: When Moses realized that God's decree about his death had been sealed, he drew a circle in the dirt, stood inside it and shouted:

Moses: Ruler-of-the-Universe, I will not move out of this circle until You change Your mind and take back the decree.

Narrator: He put on sackcloth and ashes and stood praying and petitioning God. Soon heaven, earth and all of creation were shaking. Everyone was afraid that God was going to destroy the world and start again.

God: Close the gates of heaven. Do not let Moses' prayers and requests enter. I do not want to hear them.

Narrator: But Moses' cries began to cut through the heavenly gates like a blowtorch. God ordered the ministering angels:

God: Bolt every gate in heaven!

Moses: Ruler-of-the-Universe! You know all the pain and suffering I endured until the Families of Israel believed in You. You know how hard it was to teach them Torah and the mitzvot. All I want is to see a little of their happiness after all those years of pain in the wilderness. Is that too much to ask? Yet now You tell me, "You shall not pass over the Jordan." Oh, God! In that case Your Torah is a lie—it is unjust—because Your own law says: "AN EMPLOYER IS COMMANDED TO PAY HIS HIRED SERVANT ON THE DAY HE FINISHES WORK" *(Leviticus 19:13)*. So how come I had to work for forty years to try to get Israel to be a holy and faithful nation, and I get nothing?

God: This is still my decree!

SCENE 2: MOSES PLAYS "LET'S MAKE A DEAL"

Moses: If You won't let me enter the Promised Land alive, then how about letting me be brought in dead, like Joseph's bones?

God: Moses, when Joseph went down to Egypt he did not hide the fact that he was a Hebrew. He told everyone about his Jewish identity. However, when you arrived in Midian you let people think you were an Egyptian.

Moses: Well, if You won't bring me into the Land, then at least let me be like one of the beasts of the field that eats grass, drinks the stream waters and looks out at the world.

God: Stop! Enough! No!

Moses: Then let me fly like a bird that goes searching in all directions for its food and then comes back to its nest at day's end.

God: Enough already! Stop! No more!

SCENE 3: A FRIEND IN NEED

Narrator: Next Moses turned to the heavens and the earth.

Moses: Intercede for me. Help me to change God's mind.

Heavens & Earth: We have ourselves to worry about. Our time is limited, too. We've been warned. Remember?

Bible: THE HEAVENS SHALL DISAPPEAR LIKE SMOKE, AND THE EARTH SHALL WEAR OUT LIKE OLD CLOTHES *(Isaiah 51:6)*.

Narrator: Then Moses asked the sun, moon and stars to help.

Moses: Pray for me!

Sun, Moon, Stars: We've got our own worries. We will die, too. We've been warned, too. Listen:

Bible: ALL OF THE OBJECTS OF HEAVEN SHALL BE DISSOLVED *(Isaiah 34:4)*.

Narrator: Moses went to the mountains and hills.

Moses: Pray for me!

Mountains & Hills: We can't help you—we first have to beg for ourselves. We've got to save ourselves. We've been warned as well:

Bible: FOR THE MOUNTAINS WILL DEPART, AND THE HILLS WILL BE REMOVED *(Isaiah 54:10)*.

Narrator: Next on Moses' list was the sea.

Moses: Pray for mercy for me.

The Sea: Son of Amram, what makes today different than yesterday? Aren't you the same son of Amram who beat me with his staff and divided me into twelve tiny streams? I had no way of defending myself against you, because you stood at God's right hand. I had nowhere I could go for help. Now the tables are turned; you come and ask me to help you. Why should I help you?

Moses: Would that I were back in the old days. I used to stand by the Reed Sea as if I were a king—but now I cry for help, and no one listens to me.

Narrator: Next Moses sneaked into heaven and cornered one of the ministering angels.

Moses: I beg of you—please pray for mercy for me.

Angel: Moses, my teacher, why are you going to all this bother? It can't do any good. I already know from the Inner Court that your prayers will not be heard on this matter.

SCENE 4: SOLO, THE FACE-TO-FACE

Narrator: Moses places his hands on his head and starts to cry.

Moses: To whom can I go? Who will intercede with God to have mercy on me?

Narrator: God was getting angrier and angrier with Moses. The more he begged, the angrier God got. That is until Moses prayed with the words:

Moses: THE ETERNAL, THE ETERNAL THE GOD, THE MERCIFUL, THE GRACIOUS (Exodus 34:6).

Narrator: Right away God's anger subsided. God again spoke to Moses:

God: Moses, do you remember that I took two oaths? The first was to destroy Israel after they had worshiped the Golden Calf. The second was that you would die and not enter the Promised Land. I gave up and canceled the first oath when you prayed. Now you want Me to forget My second oath. You are holding onto both ends of the rope; it doesn't work that way. If you want Me to answer this prayer, then I will restore the first oath and destroy Israel. Otherwise, if you want that oath to remain in effect, you must withdraw your present prayer.

Moses: Ruler-of-the-Universe, better Moses and a thousand like him have to die before a single fingernail on one Israelite be hurt.

Ruler-of-the-Universe! Are You really going to let the feet that came up on high and the face that looked face-to-face with God and the hands that received the Torah directly from You sleep in the dirt?

God: That is My plan, and that is the law of life. Each generation will have its own teachers and its own leaders. Until now you've been the one to serve Me. From now on that will be Joshua your servant's responsibility.

Moses: Ruler-of-the-Universe, I have to die because it's Joshua's turn to become the leader. Why not just let me be his disciple?

God: If that is what you want to do, go and do it.

SCENE 5: MOSES, THE SERVANT OF JOSHUA

Narrator: So Moses got up early in the morning and went to the door of Joshua's tent. Joshua was seated, busy teaching Torah. Moses quietly entered with his hand on his heart. Joshua was focused on his teaching and didn't notice Moses. Meanwhile, many Israelites had gone to Moses' tent door, wanting to study Torah with him. They asked:

Israelites: Where is Moses our teacher?

Narrator: They were told that he had gone to Joshua's tent. They followed and found him standing there while Joshua sat and taught Torah.

Israelites: Joshua! What is the meaning of this? How can you sit and teach while Moses is standing?

Narrator: Joshua raised his eyes and saw Moses standing. He cried:

Joshua: Rabbi, Rabbi, Father, Father!

Israelites: Moses, teach us Torah.

Moses: I am not permitted.

Israelites: We will not abandon you!

Moses: From now on you must learn Torah from Joshua.

Narrator: They accepted this command and sat down to hear the teachings of Joshua. Joshua sat at the head, Moses at his right hand and the sons of Aaron at his left. Joshua taught Torah in the presence of Moses, his teacher. This is the way the mantle of authority and wisdom passed from Moses to Joshua. Later Moses and Joshua went to the Mishkan. There the cloud of the Shekhinah came down and divided them. Then it was gone.

Moses: What did God have to say?

Joshua: I am not allowed to tell you, just as you were not permitted to tell me everything when God used to speak to you.

Moses: Better one thousand deaths than a single jealousy! Oh Ruler-of-the-Universe, up to now I sought life, but now I am ready to return my soul to You!

SCENE 6: MEANWHILE, BACK IN HEAVEN...

God: WHO WILL NOW RISE UP FOR ME AGAINST EVIL DOERS? *(Psalm 94:16)*. Who will now defend Israel against My anger? Who will stand by to pray for them when they are at war? Who will seek My mercy when they sin against Me?

Narrator: The first to speak was Metatron, God's personal ministering angel and Israel's number-one advocate. Metatron was the angel who kept the book of Israel's good deeds.

Metatron: Ruler-of-the-Universe! Moses is now dying in accordance with Your law. Why then do You mourn?

God: Let me tell you a story: Once there was a king of flesh and blood who had a son who angered him by his wild and rebellious behavior. In fact, the king often got so angry that he wanted to kill the son but was prevented from doing so by the queen, who saved her son. Then the queen died, and the king deeply mourned her. When his ministers asked the reason for the depth of his sadness, he answered, "I am not only mourning for my wife, but also for my son. Many times I have been so angry with him that I would have killed him, if not for his mother. His mother saved him every time." This is exactly how I feel. I am mourning not only for Moses but for Israel, because every time they angered Me, Moses stood by them, defended them and took away My anger.

Narrator: God then spoke to Gabriel, the angel who guards paradise and will eventually blow the great shofar:

God: Go and bring home the soul of Moses.

Gabriel: Ruler-of-the-Universe, how can I be witness to the death of one who is the equal of the six hundred thousand Israelites?

Narrator: So then God turned to Michael, another one of the four angels in God's inner circle. He was the commando angel who always defended Israel. He was the angel who taught Moses Torah.

God: Go and bring home the soul of Moses.

Michael: I was his teacher, and he was my pupil. How can I bring about his death?

Narrator: Finally God turned to Sammael, the chief of the angels who worked for Satan, the prosecuting angel. He was the angel of death. Now Sammael had been waiting hourly for Moses' death and had been asking:

Sammael: When will the moment come when I will be able to take away his soul? When will I get to see Michael weep as my mouth fills with joy?

God: Go and bring home the soul of Moses.

Narrator: When God finally gave him the command, he clothed himself in anger, put on his sword, wrapped himself in his cloak of terror and went out to Moses.

SCENE 7: MOSES VS SAMMAEL

Narrator: When Sammael came to Moses, Moses was busy writing God's name in a sefer Torah. Moses glowed with light. He was as bright as the sun. He looked a lot like an angel. Sammael was afraid. He was terrified. He couldn't speak.

Moses: Wicked one, what are you doing here?

Sammael: I have come to take away your soul.

Moses: Who sent you?

Sammael: The One-Who-Created-All-Things.

Moses: Get away from here. I wish to praise the Holy-One-Who-Is-to-Be-Praised: "I SHALL NOT DIE BUT LIVE IF I TELL OF GOD'S WORKS" *(Psalm 118:17)*.

Sammael: Don't be so high and mighty. God already has someone to sing praises: "THE HEAVENS DECLARE THE GLORY OF GOD" *(Psalm 19:2)*.

Moses: I can shut them up. "HEAVENS, LISTEN AND I WILL SPEAK. LET THE EARTH HEAR THE WORDS OF MY MOUTH" *(Deuteronomy 32:1)*.

Sammael: But all living things must return their souls to me!

Moses: Yes, but I have more power than any other living thing.

Sammael: What is your power?

Moses: I am the son of Amram, who at the age of three prophesied that I would receive the Torah in the midst of flames. I went into a king's place and removed the crown from the king's head. When I was eighty I performed signs and miracles in Egypt and brought out six hundred thousand Jews despite the might of Egypt. I divided the sea; I climbed up and made a way to heaven. I fought a battle with the angels who didn't want me to receive the Torah. I spoke to God face to face and received the Torah from God's right hand and taught it to Israel. I also caused the sun and the moon to stand still in heaven. Who else in all the world has done such things? Go away. I will not give my soul to you.

Narrator: Sammael went back to God and told him what had happened.

God: Go back and bring the soul of Moses back here.

Narrator: Sammael unsheathed his sword and stood at Moses' side. Moses became angry with him. He took his staff with God's name inscribed on it. He hit Sammael with all his might, and the angel fled. Moses continued to chase him away. Then Moses took a beam of light from between his eyes and blinded the angel of death.

SCENE 8: GOD STEPS IN

God: Moses, the hour has come. You must now depart from the world.

Moses: Ruler-of-the-Universe. Remember when You appeared to me from the burning bush. Do you remember how I stood on Mt. Sinai for forty days and forty nights? I beg You, do not deliver me into the hands of the angel of death.

God: Fear not, Moses. I Myself will attend to you and bury you.

Moses: All right, but please give me a couple of moments. I want to bless Israel. All these years they have only gotten orders, warnings and scoldings from me.

Narrator: So Moses began to bless each tribe separately. When he saw that the hour was drawing to a close he united the tribes for a single blessing.

Moses: I have troubled you much with the Torah and the mitzvot. Now forgive me.

Israelites: Moses, our teacher and our leader, you are forgiven.

Narrator: Then the people drew close to him.

Israelites: We have frequently made you very angry and given you much distress. Forgive us!

Moses: You are forgiven.

God: The moment has arrived for you to depart from this world.

Moses: Bless the Name of The One Who lives and exists forever.

Narrator: He then turned back to the Israelites and said:

Moses: Please, when you enter the Land, remember me and my bones and say, "Alas for the son of Amram, who ran bravely before us but whose bones fell in the wilderness."

God: Now you must depart from the world.

Moses: Now you see the destiny of all living things.

Narrator: Moses sanctified himself like the angels. Then God descended with his four closest ministering angels from the highest heaven to retrieve the soul of Moses. The angels stood around Moses.

God: Moses, close your eyes. Now place your hands on your breast. Bring your feet together. Precious soul, I set a time of one hundred and twenty years for you to be in the body of Moses. Now the time has come for you to depart. Please leave the body—do not wait.

Moses' Soul: Ruler-of-the-Universe. I know that You are the God of all spirits and the Master of all souls. You created me and placed me in the body of Moses for one hundred and twenty years. Now I ask, is there a better body in the entire world than that of Moses? I love him, and I don't want to leave him.

God: Come with Me, and I will raise you to the highest heaven and set you down beneath the throne of my glory—right alongside the cherubim and seraphim.

Narrator: At that moment God kissed Moses and removed his soul with a kiss. Then God wept:

God: THERE HAS NEVER ARISEN IN ISRAEL SINCE THEN ANOTHER PROPHET WHO CAN BE COMPARED TO MOSES *(Deuteronomy 34:10)*.

Narrator: And the heavens wept:

Heavens: THE GODLY MAN IS PERISHED FROM THE EARTH *(Micah 7:2)*.

Narrator: The earth wept:

Earth: AND THE MOST UPRIGHT AMONG MEN IS NO MORE *(Micah 7:2)*.

Narrator: The ministering angels wept:

Angels: HE DID THE ETERNAL'S JUSTICE *(Deuteronomy 33:21)*.

Narrator: Israel wept:

Israelites: HE BROUGHT THE ETERNAL'S JUDGMENT TO ISRAEL *(Deuteronomy 33:21)*.

All: HE ENTERS INTO PEACE. EVERY ONE THAT WALKS IN RIGHTEOUSNESS RESTS PEACEFULLY *(Isaiah 57:2)*.

ḤEVRUTA LEARNING

The Torah is an ancient text, and it has come down the line of our ancestors all the way to us over some 3000 years! The rabbis of the Mishnah identified the chain of the tradition by which the Torah passed from Moses to the rabbis and from the rabbis to us. They recorded it in the verse line of *Pirkei Avot*, a book of wise teachings:

> Moses received the Torah at Mount Sinai and transmitted it to Joshua, Joshua to the elders, and the elders to the prophets, and the prophets to the Members of the Great Assembly. They said three things: Be patient in justice, raise many disciples, and make a fence round the Torah. (Pirkei Avot 1:1)

Reflection Question: What does it mean to build a fence around the Torah?

MITZVAH OF THE WEEK: WRITE YOURSELF A TORAH

A few *parashiyot* ago, we learned. "Write this song for yourself" *(Deuteronomy 31.19).*

This is the last mitzvah in the Torah. Every Jew is supposed to write their own Torah. If you do not know how, you can pay someone to do it for you.

When you write a sefer Torah:

- you must write it by hand.
- you must write it on sheets of parchment.
- you must write it in Hebrew.
- you must start with a meditation.
- you must sew the sheet together with sinews of clean animals.
- you must copy it from a kosher sefer Torah.
- you must pronounce every word before you write it.

K' TUV כְּתוֹב לְכֶם אֶת הַשִּׁירָה הַזֹּאת *LEKHEM ET HA-SHIRAH HA-ZOT* EXPERIENCE

There are stories about Jews in the former Soviet Union who recreated books and history from memory. They would ask every visitor to fill in a piece.

Work as a committee without any resources and write down as much of the Torah as you can from memory.

Reflection Question: Why does the Torah want every Jew to write their own copy of the Torah?